The Moonstone

This is a work of fiction. All of the characters, events, and organizations portrayed in this work are either products of the authors' imagination or used fictitiously.

The Moonstone

Copyright © 2011 by Robert Kauzlaric

Based on the novel by Wilkie Collins published in 1868.

Cover by David Blixt

All rights reserved. No part of this book may be reproduced in any form by any electronic or mechanical means including photocopying, recording, or information storage and retrieval without permission in writing from the author.

ISBN-13: 978-0692251348
ISBN-10: 0692251340

For information about production rights, e-mail:
rob@lifelinetheatre.com

Published by Sordelet Ink

The Moonstone

Adapted for the Stage by
Robert Kauzlaric

From the Novel by
Wilkie Collins

Published by
Sordelet Ink

The Moonstone received its world premiere at Lifeline Theatre in Chicago, IL, on February 14, 2011. It was directed by Paul S. Holmquist; sound design was by Cristina DeRisi; costume design was by Bill Morey; violence design was by R&D Choreography (Richard Gilbert and David Gregory); properties design was by Joe Schermoly; lighting design was by Brandon Wardell; scenic design was by Ian Zywica; and the production stage manager was Katie Adams. The cast was as follows:

Rosanna Spearman/Drusilla Clack - Kaitlin Byrd
Penelope Betteredge/Woman - Sonja Field
Indian #1/Ezra Jennings - Peter Greenberg
Matthew Bruff/Thomas Candy - Vincent P. Mahler
Godfrey Ablewhite - C. Sean Piereman
Franklin Blake - Cody Proctor
Mr. Murthwaite/Septimus Luker - John Henry Roberts
Gabriel Betteredge - Sean Sinitski
Col. John Herncastle/Sgt. Richard Cuff/
Mr. Ablewhite, Sr - Dave Skvarla
Rachel Verinder - Ann Sonneville
Lady Julia Verinder/Landlady - Jenifer Tyler

Understudies - Vic May, Jhenai Mootz

The following credit must appear in all programs/playbills handed to audience members at performances of The Moonstone:

The Moonstone was originally produced by Lifeline Theatre, Chicago, Illinois, and premiered there in 2011.

Cast of Characters

RACHEL VERINDER – *A beautiful and self-willed young heiress.*
LADY JULIA VERINDER – *A kind and generous mother and mistress; secretly afflicted with heart disease.*
DRUSILLA CLACK – *A long-suffering woman, concerned with the salvation of those around her.*
PENELOPE BETTEREDGE – *A feisty and quick-witted young maid.*
ROSANNA SPEARMAN – *A reformed criminal with a deformed shoulder.*
WOMAN – *A nervous woman at Luker's bank.*
LANDLADY – *Of 'The Wheel of Fortune.'*

MR. MURTHWAITE – *A dashing world traveler and London celebrity.*
FRANKLIN BLAKE – *An earnest young man with a mercurial temperament.*
GODFREY ABLEWHITE – *A self-assured ladies' man and philanthropist.*
THOMAS CANDY – *A country doctor; socially clumsy.*
COLONEL JOHN HERNCASTLE – *A fierce, bitter blackguard.*
INDIAN #1 – *The leader of the guardian priests; a tormented soul yearning for release.*
INDIANS #2 and #3 – *Typically seen in linen ceremonial frocks which obscure their faces.*
GABRIEL BETTEREDGE – *Lifelong servant to the Verinder family; distinguished and devoted.*
MATTHEW BRUFF – *The Verinder family lawyer; practical but sincere.*
SERGEANT RICHARD CUFF – *The finest police detective in England; an amateur gardener.*
EZRA JENNINGS – *A tortured gypsy with piebald hair; a doctor's assistant and opium addict.*
SEPTIMUS LUKER – *A sniveling, cowardly moneylender.*
MR. ABLEWHITE, senior – *A proud, self-made businessman with a roaring temper.*

The roles of INDIAN #2 and #3 may be shared by the ensemble, always appearing concealed by their ceremonial robes. Other roles, as needed, are played by the ensemble: servants, Londoners, etc.

ACT I

Darkness. An idol of the moon god appears above the stage, the Moonstone glowing from its forehead. Three robed INDIANS worship at its feet. A light rises on RACHEL, the Moonstone gleaming from the bodice of her dress. Lights expand to reveal LADY JULIA, FRANKLIN, GODFREY, CLACK, CANDY, and MURTHWAITE gathered around a table.

MURTHWAITE
Since antiquity, Hindu myth describes a precious stone set in the forehead of the Indian moon god. Owing to its peculiar color, and a superstition that its luster waxes and wanes with the lunar cycle, this gem gained the name of the Moonstone.

INDIAN #1
Vishnu the Preserver has commanded that the Moonstone shall be watched, by three priests, night and day, to the end of time.

MURTHWAITE
These priests, generations of them, sacrificed everything to protect the ancient stone, in service to their god.

INDIAN #1
And know that Lord Vishnu predicts the certain disaster of any mortal to lay his hands on the sacred gem.

MURTHWAITE
The threat of this curse kept it safe for hundreds of years. But, in time, the world grew smaller, and man's violent ambitions grew large. An invading army seized the stone and the three priests pursued, bent on recovering it.

(The stone vanishes from the forehead of the idol)

MURTHWAITE
The Moonstone fell from army to army, tyrant to tyrant; always passing in bloodshed and misery. And for generations, the successors of the three priests kept their watch. Then in 1799, the British army stormed Seringapatam. The streets were thick with the slain; blood flowed like the sacred river. And inside a hidden armory, the sacred diamond was finally recovered by its guardians, only to be seized by a renegade British officer...

(HERNCASTLE enters to discover the INDIANS with the Moonstone)

MURTHWAITE
Colonel John Herncastle. *(To RACHEL)* Your uncle, miss. Now, I give no credence to the notion of a curse, but it is my conviction that crime brings its own fatality with it.

(HERNCASTLE ruthlessly slays two of the INDIANS and mortally wounds the third)

INDIAN #1
The Moonstone will have its vengeance on you and yours! *(He dies)*

(HERNCASTLE takes up the Moonstone)

RACHEL
What happened to the Colonel, mamma?

LADY JULIA
We had hoped to leave the Colonel and his wickedness behind us. But you cannot hide from your past. My brother was called Honorable John, but he was, I believe, one of the greatest blackguards that ever lived. After India, he fell into ruin. His life was threatened repeatedly, owing to the conspiracy surrounding the Moonstone. His character was so degraded that he drove the family away and vowed vengeance upon us all. John was once my beloved brother, but the man who stole that diamond was a man I did not know. A man none could trust. Even on his deathbed.

(Lights fade on all but HERNCASTLE)

HERNCASTLE
The fortunes of war have placed me in possession of one of the largest diamonds in the world and I wish to see it remain within the bosom of my family. I hereby bequeath to my niece, Rachel Verinder – only if her mother be living on Rachel's next birthday – the yellow diamond known in the East as the Moonstone. I give the diamond in token of my free forgiveness of her mother's conduct towards me in

my lifetime. May it bring them all they deserve. *(He exits)*

(Lights rise on FRANKLIN, who carries a journal)

FRANKLIN
(To the audience) There can be no doubt that our strange family story must be told. We are all prisoners of the past; players in a story far larger than any of us. But the time has come to tell our part in the tale of the Moonstone, and to lay this matter to rest for once and all. My name is Franklin Blake.

(BETTEREDGE enters, led by PENELOPE. CLACK, BRUFF, and CUFF follow)

BETTEREDGE
(To the audience) Gabriel Betteredge, house–steward in service of the Verinder family.

PENELOPE
(To the audience) His daughter, Penelope.

CLACK
(To the audience) Drusilla Clack, a poor Christian compelled by my wealthy relative – would I could say spiritually wealthy! – to reopen wounds that Time has barely healed.

BRUFF
(To the audience) Matthew Bruff, the family solicitor.

CUFF
(To the audience) I am Sergeant Cuff, formerly of the Detective Police.

(FRANKLIN removes a letter from within the journal and places it in a prominent place onstage. He then places the journal itself in another location, with rever-

ence. As he does so, lights rise on MURTHWAITE and JENNINGS)

FRANKLIN
(To the audience) And others will join us through written testimonial. Now, I believe I have hit on the right way of doing this. We have certain events to relate, and certain persons who are uniquely capable of doing so. We shall tell the story of the Moonstone in turn, each revealing the part of the story we know best, and only as far as our personal knowledge extended at the time.

BETTEREDGE
But, given what we now know—

FRANKLIN
Forget what you know. We will share what happened. This is to be a record of our observations, not our regrets or conjecture. *(To the audience)* We shall attempt, as best we can, to reconstruct the truth of the matter; though I am painfully aware that there may not be an objective Truth to be found.

CUFF
I beg to differ, Mr. Blake. We have an abundance of evidence at our disposal.

BETTEREDGE
We have fragments, personal experiences; all biased and flawed.

BRUFF
Criminals have been sentenced to death with far less.

FRANKLIN
We are not judges, gentlemen. We are merely players

in a story with its roots in legend and its conclusion yet untold. But, let us begin. *(To the audience)* The first thing is to tell how the diamond found its way into my aunt's house in Yorkshire, and how it came to be lost twelve hours later. Nobody knows as much as our faithful servant Betteredge about what went on at that time. So he will begin our story.

(Lights fade on all but BETTEREDGE as PENELOPE urges him forward)

BETTEREDGE
As you say, sir. *(To the audience)* In the first part of Robinson Crusoe, it is written: "Now I saw, though too late, the Folly of beginning a Work before we count the Cost, and before we judge rightly of our own Strength to go through with it." Only yesterday, I opened my copy by accident at that place. Now, allow me to ask: if that isn't prophecy, what is? Such a book will never be written again. I have turned to it for years, often with a pipe of tobacco, and found it a friend in need. When my spirits are bad: Robinson Crusoe. When I want advice: Robinson Crusoe—

PENELOPE
(Joining BETTEREDGE) Father, this doesn't sound like the story of the diamond, now does it? Just lay out what happened, beginning with the morning we got the news of Mr. Franklin. You know, if you need help, I keep a diary with all the dates we need…

BETTEREDGE
Perhaps you should tell the story, then, out of your diary.

PENELOPE
My journal is private, and no one shall ever know what is in it but myself!

BETTEREDGE
(To the audience) We all know what that means: sweethearts.

PENELOPE
Fiddlesticks! Start again.

(LADY JULIA and RACHEL appear in the Verinder sitting room as BETTEREDGE names them)

BETTEREDGE
(To the audience) If you know anything of the fashionable world, you have heard of Lady Julia Verinder and her daughter, Miss Rachel. I have served their family all my days, and my lady saw to it that my little girl Penelope was taken care of, and promoted to be Miss Rachel's maid. On a spring day in 1848…

LADY JULIA
Gabriel, I have wonderful news. Franklin has returned from abroad. He arrives tomorrow to stop till next month, and keep Rachel's birthday.

BETTEREDGE
I have not seen Master Franklin since he was a boy! He was, out of all sight, the nicest lad that ever spun a top or broke a window.

RACHEL
Funny, I remember him as the most atrocious tyrant that ever tortured a doll.

BETTEREDGE
(To the audience) You will naturally be curious about

Mr. Franklin, and how he should have passed all the years, from boyhood to manhood, out of his own country.

(FRANKLIN appears as lights fade on LADY JULIA and RACHEL)

BETTEREDGE
(To the audience) Franklin Blake is my lady's nephew. His father refused to let England educate the boy and sent him to institutions abroad.

FRANKLIN
(To the audience) I learnt what the Germans could teach me; I gave the French a turn next, and the Italians a turn after that.

BETTEREDGE
(To the audience) They made him a sort of universal genius.

FRANKLIN
(To the audience) Well, I don't know about that...

BETTEREDGE
(To the audience) His mother's fortune fell to him when he came of age, and ran through him as through a sieve. There was a hole in his pocket that nothing would sew up. He lived here, there, and everywhere; his address, he used to say, was...

FRANKLIN
(To the audience) "Post Office, Europe: to be left till called for." *(He exits)*

BETTEREDGE
(To the audience) So, we were finally to see what our nice boy had grown to be as a man. That day, I was

going about my work when I heard a noise from the back terrace.

(BETTEREDGE encounters INDIANS #1, #2 and #3 sneaking into the back of the house)

BETTEREDGE
Who are you? How did you get in here?

INDIAN #1
(As they pull out hand drums and begin to play) We are strolling jugglers and conjurors, good sir. With your permission, I request to show our tricks in the presence of the lady of the house.

BETTEREDGE
I am all for amusement, and the last person to distrust another because he is a few shades darker than myself. But the lady of the house is out; and I must warn you off the premises.

INDIAN #1
As you wish, sir. Our blessing upon you. *(He bows and departs with the other INDIANS)*

BETTEREDGE
(To the audience) I thought no more of the encounter until Master Franklin's arrival—

(PENELOPE enters)

PENELOPE
But, wait, father. *(To the audience)* That wasn't the last we saw of the Indians. I was on the road from Frizinghall when I spied them passing by. So, I stole along the side of the hedge....

(Observed by PENELOPE, the INDIANS gather in the shadows alongside the road. INDIAN #1 draws

forth a bottle and pours black ink into INDIAN #2's hands and makes signs in the air)

INDIAN #1
Look. *(INDIAN #2 becomes as stiff as a statue, staring wide-eyed into the palm of his hand)* Do you see the English gentleman from foreign parts? *(INDIAN #2 nods)* Is it on this road that he will travel today? *(INDIAN #2 nods)* Has he got It about him?

INDIAN #2
Yes.

(Lights fade on the INDIANS as PENELOPE returns to BETTEREDGE)

PENELOPE
(To the audience) I told my father at once. *(To BETTEREDGE)* Isn't it dreadful? You must do something!

BETTEREDGE
They must have heard of Mr. Franklin's arrival from the gardener, and thought to make a little money by it. They were simply practicing their hocus-pocus, like actors rehearsing a play.

PENELOPE
This is serious! Ask Mr. Franklin if he thinks it a laughing matter! *(She starts to exit)*

BETTEREDGE
Where are you off to now, young lady?

PENELOPE
Rosanna's late for dinner, and I'm to fetch her in. Again.

BETTEREDGE

Where is she?

PENELOPE
At the sands, of course! I have no patience with her!

BETTEREDGE
I have patience with her; I'll fetch her in. *(To the audience)* So, I set off at once.

PENELOPE
No; wait; they must hear more of the Shivering Sand, and of Rosanna, first.

BETTEREDGE
Ah, yes; of course!

PENELOPE
(To the audience) But we'll find ourselves in the thick of the mystery soon, I promise you!

(ROSANNA and LADY JULIA appear)

BETTEREDGE
(To the audience) My lady had recently been in London to visit a Reformatory, intending to save women from drifting back into bad ways after prison. There she met Rosanna Spearman.

LADY JULIA
(To ROSANNA) I know you were a thief, Rosanna, but you have paid your debt to society. My opinion is that you only want a chance to prove yourself worthy; and you shall have your chance, in my service. Join my staff as our second housemaid. Not a soul will be told your story, excepting Mr. Betteredge.

BETTEREDGE

(To the audience) A fairer chance no one could have had. In return, Rosanna showed herself worthy. But she failed to make friends among the other women servants. She certainly had no beauty to make them envious; but I think they resented her solitary ways.

PENELOPE
The sands, father? *(To the audience)* Our house is in Yorkshire, close by the sea. We've got lovely walks all round us, except one which leads to the loneliest and ugliest bay on all our coast.

(Lights rise on ROSANNA standing alone above the Shivering Sand)

PENELOPE
(To the audience) There lies the most horrible quicksand in England. At the turn of the tide, something goes on in the deeps, which sets the face of the sand trembling, giving it the name of the Shivering Sand. A horrid retreat! Yet still, this was Rosanna's favorite walk.

(PENELOPE exits. BETTEREDGE joins ROSANNA, who is crying. BETTEREDGE offers a handkerchief)

BETTEREDGE
Now, now, Rosanna. *(He dries ROSANNA's eyes)* What are you crying about, my dear?

ROSANNA
My past still comes back to me sometimes.

BETTEREDGE
Those days have been washed away. Why can't you forget them?

ROSANNA

How can I forget my own life, Mr. Betteredge?

BETTEREDGE
Come now, my girl. The table has been set.

ROSANNA
Please let me bide a little longer.

BETTEREDGE
What is it that brings you to this miserable place?

ROSANNA
I think it has laid a spell on me. I dream of it night after night. You know I am grateful; that I try to deserve your kindness, and my lady's confidence in me. But I wonder whether life here is too good for a woman like me. Look at the quicksand! Do you know how it appears to me? Like there are people beneath it, struggling to get to the surface, but all sinking into the deeps!

FRANKLIN
(Offstage) Dear old Betteredge!

ROSANNA
(Her color changes abruptly) Oh! Who is that?

(FRANKLIN enters)

BETTEREDGE
Master Franklin!

FRANKLIN
(Giving BETTEREDGE a vigorous hug) Ah, my dear friend, it's been far too long! What are you doing in this wretched place? *(To ROSANNA)* And who is this?

(ROSANNA exits suddenly, without a word)
FRANKLIN

That's an odd girl. Well, I'm glad we're alone, actually. We must discuss the Indians you saw today. Don't look so surprised; Penelope told me. Your daughter promised to be a pretty girl, Betteredge, and she has kept her promise.

BETTEREDGE
(Changing the subject with a dark look at FRANKLIN)
The Indians, sir?

FRANKLIN
Ah, yes. 'Has the English gentleman got It about him?' they said. *(Pulling forth a sealed paper parcel)* I suspect that 'It' means this: my uncle Herncastle's famous diamond.

BETTEREDGE
How do you come to be in charge of the wicked Colonel's gem?

FRANKLIN
The wicked Colonel's Will left it as a birthday present to Rachel, and I have been charged with bringing it to her. But listen to this: when I took the diamond from the bank, I was followed by men in Indian garb. The next day, I saw them again. I come here, and what is the first news that meets me? Three Indians have been expecting my arrival.

BETTEREDGE
Good Lord, sir!

FRANKLIN
You know my uncle's dark history. You know he believed that the gem was the object of a violent conspiracy. What do you think? Did he purposely leave a legacy of danger to Aunt Julia, through

Rachel?

BETTEREDGE
It seems dreadful to believe, sir, that he died with revenge in his heart, and a horrid lie on his lips. God alone knows the truth. Don't ask me.

FRANKLIN
Dear Betteredge, instruct me. Should I tell my aunt what has happened? I don't want to alarm her without reason. What should I do?

BETTEREDGE
Well, we've got four weeks before Miss Rachel's birthday. Why not wait and see what happens in that time; and warn my lady, or not, as circumstances direct us. In the meantime, keep it safe in the bank at Frizinghall.

FRANKLIN
Perfect! Betteredge, you are worth your weight in gold! *(He exits)*

BETTEREDGE
(To the audience) Here, God bless it, was the Master Franklin I remembered. He raced off at once to lodge the cursed diamond in the strong room of the bank.

(BETTEREDGE crosses to meet PENELOPE. ROSANNA is seen in dumb show, staring in a mirror)

PENELOPE
What happened with Rosanna, father?

BETTEREDGE
Whatever do you mean?

PENELOPE

She returned to the house asking hundreds of questions about Mr. Franklin. Then I found her later, crying into the glass. You know what I think? Rosanna has fallen in love with Mr. Franklin at first sight! Imagine that: a housemaid with a plain face, mooning over a gentleman!

BETTEREDGE
This cruelty does not become you, my girl.

(PENELOPE exits)

BETTEREDGE
(To the audience) I had hoped to see Penelope's prejudice soften over time. If only poor Rosanna had had a single friend in our house, perhaps...

(RACHEL and FRANKLIN appear in the sitting room, and ROSANNA disappears)

BETTEREDGE
(To the audience) Well, we should carry on. That evening, Mr. Franklin met Miss Rachel for the first time since childhood.

FRANKLIN
(To BETTEREDGE) I tell you, Betteredge, Rachel's quite put that silly diamond clean out of my head. She's the most charming girl I've ever met!

(FRANKLIN and RACHEL work on the door during the following, while PENELOPE attends)

BETTEREDGE
(To the audience) To pass the month before Miss Rachel's birthday, they devoted themselves to making a mess, dabbling in what Mr. Franklin called "decorative painting."

RACHEL

(Smelling a substance in one of FRANKLIN's jars)
Oh, how dreadful! What is this?

FRANKLIN
In Italy, I lived with the most wonderful old painter; brilliant with oils. Under his tutelage, I invented a new vehicle for moistening paint. Works quite well, if I say so myself.

RACHEL
Modest as ever, aren't you?

FRANKLIN
How shall we decorate the door?

RACHEL
I rather fancy those griffins and cupids by that... famous Italian painter who did all the Virgin Maries, and had a sweetheart at the baker's. You know the one...

FRANKLIN
Ah, there is so much to teach you.

BETTEREDGE
(To the audience) Who was it that said, "Satan finds mischief for idle hands to do?"

PENELOPE
Oh, father; hush. *(To the audience)* We all speculated that there would be a wedding in the house before the summer was over.

BETTEREDGE
(To the audience) But some, led by me, wondered if the bridegroom would be Mr. Franklin. An invitation from my mistress was sent to another gentleman, to come and keep Miss Rachel's birthday. This

was the man on whom I believed her heart to be set. Like Mr. Franklin, he was a cousin of hers. His name: Godfrey Ablewhite.

(GODFREY appears)

BETTEREDGE
(To the audience) He was a barrister by profession; a ladies' man by temperament; and a good Samaritan by choice. Wherever there was a committee of women, there was Mr. Godfrey leading the dear creatures along the thorny ways of business, hat in hand. He was the most accomplished philanthropist England ever produced.

PENELOPE
(To the audience) He loved everybody. And everybody loved him.

BETTEREDGE
(To the audience) What chance had Mr. Franklin against such a man as he?

PENELOPE
(To the audience) Mr. Godfrey accepted Lady Julia's invitation by letter.

(ROSANNA enters and hands a letter to RACHEL)

GODFREY
It is my pleasure to accept your kind invitation. I can stay through Friday, when my duties to the Ladies' Charities oblige me to return to town. Please note that I have enclosed a set of handwritten verses – mere fancies, I'm sure – in honor of my dear cousin's natal day. *(He exits)*

FRANKLIN

"Natal day?" What an ass.

RACHEL
Now, Franklin, don't be unkind.

FRANKLIN
He's an insufferable charlatan. I don't know why Aunt Julia had to invite him.

RACHEL
What's gotten into you? You've been short-tempered for days now.

FRANKLIN
Well, if you must know... I've given up my cigars and have been sleeping very badly. Not at all, actually.

RACHEL
But you are one of the most inveterate smokers I ever met! Why did you give it up?

FRANKLIN
Because you said last week that you hated the smell of it on my clothes.

RACHEL
You didn't give up something you love on account of an idle comment from me?

FRANKLIN
I've been thinking it might be nice, actually... to spend, well, rather, the rest of my life giving things up to make you happy.

(ROSANNA *exits in tears*)

RACHEL
Oh, you silly, sleepless man. That's enough foolishness for today.
(*RACHEL and FRANKLIN exit as PENELOPE*

joins BETTEREDGE)

BETTEREDGE
(To the audience) Penelope's notion that Rosanna was in love with Mr. Franklin began to look more reasonable.

PENELOPE
(To the audience) But, we have arrived at the birthday at last! Mr. Franklin and Miss Rachel spent most of the day decorating the door, finishing by three o'clock.

BETTEREDGE
(To the audience) Then, Mr. Franklin rode to Frizinghall and returned with the diamond, and Mr. Godfrey.

(BETTEREDGE and PENELOPE cross to join LADY JULIA and RACHEL in the drawing room as GODFREY and FRANKLIN enter)

GODFREY
Dear Aunt Julia! You look as lovely as ever!

LADY JULIA
I'm so glad you've come, Godfrey.

GODFREY
As am I! And, darling Rachel! *(Kissing her hand)* Words cannot express how the sight of you lifts my poor spirits. But we've always been a comfort to each other – haven't we? – ever since childhood. Ah, Rachel! If it's not too forward of me, hasn't the time come to unite our hands in marriage? *(With a wink to LADY JULIA)* That is, if we have your blessing, Aunt Julia.

LADY JULIA

But of course you do!

RACHEL
I thank you, Godfrey, but I think it best we remain cousins, and nothing more.

GODFREY
I don't understand. Have you some personal objection to me?

RACHEL
I! I've always liked you, but—

GODFREY
Then look, for a moment, to the future. What of your happiness? I know you can be self-willed – devilish self-willed sometimes – but still, you are the finest creature that ever walked the ways of this world. Will you sentence yourself to a single life?

FRANKLIN
Godfrey, I believe you have her answer. But let's not forget the happy reason for this gathering. Rachel, I have been charged with presenting you a very special gift, in honor of your birthday...

(FRANKLIN presents the Moonstone: a large yellow diamond which glows with a life of its own. The room is captivated as FRANKLIN presses it into RACHEL's hand)

BETTEREDGE
Lord bless us!

FRANKLIN
From our uncle.

LADY JULIA

Franklin, no!

BETTEREDGE
It's... it's exquisite! It truly is!

GODFREY
Carbon! Mere carbon, nothing more! Hundreds like it, I'm sure.

RACHEL
There is nothing on earth like this.

FRANKLIN
Happy birthday, Rachel.

(RACHEL fastens the Moonstone to her dress as she, LADY JULIA, CLACK, FRANKLIN, GODFREY, CANDY, and MURTHWAITE take their places at the dinner table as at the top of the play)

BETTEREDGE
(To the audience) Soon, the rest of the dinner party arrived. Miss Rachel was naturally the great attraction of the evening, especially since – to my lady's grave concern – she wore her remarkable birthday present. Seated to her left was Mr. Candy, our doctor at Frizinghall.

CANDY
In the interests of science, Miss Rachel, you must let me take this marvelous stone home. We will heat it; then expose it to air; and – poof! – evaporate it!

BETTEREDGE
(To the audience) On Dr. Candy's left was Lady Julia's niece on her husband's side, Drusilla Clack.

CLACK

(To GODFREY, of RACHEL) Imagine! Here in Christian England, another lost soul turns to material riches for comfort!

LADY JULIA
Drusilla—

CLACK
Forgive me, Aunt Julia. I will devour my righteous indignation in silence.

BETTEREDGE
(To the audience) The guest on my young lady's right hand was none other than the celebrated world traveler, Mr. Murthwaite.

MURTHWAITE
If you ever go to India, Miss Verinder, don't take your uncle's birthday gift with you. I know a certain city where your life would not be worth five minutes' purchase.

RACHEL
What do you know of this stone?

MURTHWAITE
Since antiquity, Hindu myth describes a precious stone set in the forehead of the Indian moon god...

BETTEREDGE
(To the audience) Looking back, I believe the cursed diamond cast a blight on the whole company. Dr. Candy said more unlucky things than I ever knew him to say before.

CLACK
(To GODFREY) Professor Threadgall's wife mentioned that anatomy was his favorite subject.
CANDY

And it's so hard to find viable specimens these days, I know! Well, they've got remarkable cadavers at the College of Surgeons: organs intact, disease-free. Well, mostly—

LADY JULIA
Please, doctor, not at the table.

BETTEREDGE
(To the audience) And poor Mr. Franklin... He was still suffering from a lack of rest, and that foreign training of his came out in a most bewildering manner. Sometimes it was his French side...

FRANKLIN
(To the dinner guests) I believe there is no restriction in the lengths to which a married woman might let her admiration go for a man who is not her husband.

BETTEREDGE
(To the audience) And then he would shift to the German side...

FRANKLIN
No, hear me on this: the proper way to breed bulls is to look deep into your mind, evolve out of it the image of a perfect bull, and simply produce it!

BETTEREDGE
(To the audience) Or the Italian...

FRANKLIN
There are only three things of value in this world, I say: Love, Music, and Salad.

BETTEREDGE
(To the audience) And then things took a turn for the worse when his English side turned up and he lost

his foreign smoothness...

FRANKLIN
But on top of everything else, I have slept very badly of late.

CANDY
Your nerves are out of order. You should go through a course of medicine immediately.

FRANKLIN
A course of medicine, and a course of groping in the dark, are, in my estimation, one and the same thing.

CANDY
You are groping in the dark after sleep and nothing but medicine can help you find it.

FRANKLIN
You know, people have often told me of the blind leading the blind, and now I know what they meant.

CANDY
Sir! How dare you? What is your grievance against doctors?

(There is a crash of thunder. Then, suddenly, the doorway from the terrace is thrown open and the INDIANS enter, juggling and playing their drums. They spread out, surrounding the guests)

CLACK
Lord bless us!

LADY JULIA
What is the meaning of this?
INDIAN #1

A performance, my esteemed lady, for the celebration.

GODFREY
Who let them in?

BETTEREDGE
My lady, I told them they were not welcome here.

RACHEL
Oh, let them perform! How wonderful!

(INDIAN #1 *stops in front of* RACHEL *and looks at the Moonstone. The other two* INDIANS *close in as* INDIAN #1 *reaches out to touch the diamond)*

INDIAN #1
Not half as wonderful as this curious stone—

MURTHWAITE
Stop! *(Coming between* INDIAN #1 *and* RACHEL*)* What is the meaning of these disguises, friend?

INDIAN #1
Disguises? Whatever do you mean, good sir?

MURTHWAITE
This act of yours may fool the locals, but I know what Indian juggling really is—

INDIAN #1
Do you, now?

MURTHWAITE
Yes. And this is nothing but a clumsy imitation of it. I've spent half my life amongst your people, I'll have you know. Tell me: why have you left your homeland? Unless I'm mistaken, that is not allowed for your kind.

INDIAN #1

(A flash of fear crossing his face) Please forgive us. We meant no harm.

MURTHWAITE
Begone, I command you!

(Bowing, the INDIANS exit. FRANKLIN pulls MURTHWAITE aside during the following)

GODFREY
Well, that was exciting. Shall we retire to the drawing room, Aunt Julia?

LADY JULIA
Yes; thank you, Godfrey.

(The party exits. FRANKLIN gestures for BETTEREDGE to remain with him and MURTHWAITE)

FRANKLIN
(To MURTHWAITE) Tell Betteredge what you just told me.

MURTHWAITE
Those men are no more performers than you are; they are high-caste Brahmins; priests, I believe. They have doubly sacrificed their caste: first, in crossing the sea; secondly, in disguising themselves. This is a profound sacrifice to make. There is a serious motive at the bottom of it.

FRANKLIN
Mr. Murthwaite, may I speak to you in confidence?

BETTEREDGE
(To the audience) He told the traveler all he had told me at the Shivering Sand.

MURTHWAITE

The recovery of the Moonstone is surely behind this sacrifice of caste. Those men will await their opportunity with the patience of cats, and use it with the ferocity of tigers. You have been carrying the diamond, here and in London, and you are still alive? You are a lucky man!

BETTEREDGE
You don't mean they would have taken Mr. Franklin's life to get at their diamond?

MURTHWAITE
The sacrifice of caste is a serious thing to men of their beliefs. The sacrifice of life is nothing at all.

BETTEREDGE
Why, they are nothing but murdering thieves!

MURTHWAITE
Or is theirs a path we civilized men lack the courage to follow: abandoning everything in service to an ideal? We fight out of fear; we fight for fame or glory; but could we sacrifice ourselves purely on behalf of a belief, as they have?

FRANKLIN
They have seen the Moonstone on Rachel's dress. What's to be done?

MURTHWAITE
Send the diamond tomorrow to be cut up at Amsterdam. Make half a dozen diamonds of it, instead of one. There is an end of its sacred identity as the Moonstone, and there is an end to the conspiracy.

BETTEREDGE
But what about tonight, sir? Suppose the Indians come back?

MURTHWAITE
They won't risk it tonight.

BETTEREDGE
But suppose the rogues are bolder than you think?

MURTHWAITE
In that case, let loose the dogs. *(He exits with FRANKLIN)*

BETTEREDGE
(To the audience) It was all very well for him to joke. But my way in this world had not led me amongst thieves and murderers in all the outlandish places of the earth. In my anxiety, I turned to Robinson Crusoe, opening it at this amazing bit: "Fear of Danger is ten thousand times more terrifying than Danger itself." Any man who doesn't believe in Robinson Crusoe after that is a man with a screw loose! As for what happened in the drawing room after dinner...

(PENELOPE enters. The drawing room scene is enacted in dumb show during the following)

PENELOPE
(To the audience) It was a disaster. Lady Julia played at cards with Mr. Murthwaite and lost for the first time in my experience. Miss Rachel, engaged in conversation with that Clack woman, kept stealing glances at Mr. Franklin, who looked simply exhausted. Mr. Godfrey and Dr. Candy had their heads together like a pair of village gossips, and then the doctor disappeared for quite some time, with no word of his whereabouts.

(Rain is heard as a bell rings. The company crosses to the door, meeting CANDY, who arrives from elsewhere)

BETTEREDGE
(To the audience) With the arrival of the carriages came the arrival of the rain. Most of the company went home snugly, under cover, in closed carriages, excepting the doctor, whose gig was open to the elements.

(JENNINGS enters, his coat over his head to protect him from the rain, and stumbles into CLACK)

CLACK
(Terribly startled) Oh! Who is that?

CANDY
Don't be alarmed; it's only my assistant, Jennings.

JENNINGS
(To CANDY) I fear, sir, we'll get wet through and through on the way home.

CANDY
(Laughing) Nonsense! A doctor's skin is waterproof! You should know that, Jennings. *(He shakes hands with GODFREY and then crosses to LADY JULIA)* My thanks for an... unforgettable evening, Lady Julia.

(CANDY shakes hands with LADY JULIA and exits. CLACK and MURTHWAITE depart as well. FRANKLIN collapses on a chair)

LADY JULIA
Rachel, where are you going to put that diamond tonight?

RACHEL
I believe I shall place it in the Indian cabinet which stands in my sitting room; that way, the two beautiful native objects may admire each other.

LADY JULIA
My dear! Your cabinet has no lock to it.

RACHEL
Good Heavens, mother! Are there thieves in the house?

LADY JULIA
Why not let me keep the diamond for you tonight?

RACHEL
No, it's mine, and I shan't part with it. *(She crosses to GODFREY and offers her hand)* Godfrey.

GODFREY
Rachel. Pleasant dreams.

RACHEL
(She crosses to FRANKLIN and tidies his hair with affection) Dear Franklin, you look quite undone. Promise me you'll get some rest.

FRANKLIN
I promise.

(With a smile for FRANKLIN, RACHEL exits, followed by PENELOPE)

LADY JULIA
Gentlemen, goodnight. *(She exits)*

GODFREY
I must say, Franklin, you look like death itself. Take some brandy or something before bed.

FRANKLIN
No, no; I'm fine.

BETTEREDGE
Master Franklin, I do advise your having a nightcap.

You must get some rest tonight.

FRANKLIN
Very well. Send some brandy and water up to my room. *(He exits)*

(BETTEREDGE pours brandy and water into a glass and hands it to GODFREY, who exits with it)

BETTEREDGE
(To the audience) I sent Mr. Franklin's nightcap upstairs with Mr. Godfrey, turned out the dogs, and shut up the house. I had a touch of Mr. Franklin's malady, I believe, for I slept quite fitfully that night. Then, the next morning...

(A cry from PENELOPE sets off a cacophony of overlapping offstage voices)

PENELOPE
(Offstage) Oh, Lord!

FRANKLIN
(Offstage) Betteredge!

LADY JULIA
(Offstage) No! Not in this house!

ROSANNA
(Offstage) Find Mr. Betteredge!

FRANKLIN
(Offstage) Betteredge!

GODFREY
(Offstage) How could this happen?

(PENELOPE races in)

PENELOPE
Father! Come upstairs, for God's sake! The diamond

is gone!

BETTEREDGE
Are you out of your mind?

PENELOPE
Vanished, and nobody knows how! Come up at once!

(They cross to RACHEL's sitting room, where RACHEL stands before her open cabinet, with LADY JULIA, GODFREY, FRANKLIN, and ROSANNA looking on. FRANKLIN appears noticeably better-rested.)

PENELOPE
Look! I myself saw Miss Rachel put the diamond into that drawer last night.

BETTEREDGE
Is that true, miss?

RACHEL
Oh, God! *(Distraught, she exits into her bedroom)*

LADY JULIA
Rachel, dear! Wait! *(She follows RACHEL into her bedroom)*

GODFREY
Well. What do we do, now?

FRANKLIN
Godfrey, make sure the diamond has not accidentally dropped out of sight behind the cabinet.

(GODFREY searches around the cabinet)

FRANKLIN
Next: Penelope, tell the servants to leave the doors and windows as they were left overnight.

(PENELOPE and ROSANNA exit. LADY JULIA

reenters)

FRANKLIN
How is she, Aunt Julia?

LADY JULIA
She won't speak to me.

GODFREY
Well, it's definitely not here.

BETTEREDGE
I say; look at this! *(He points to a smear of the decorative painting on RACHEL's door)* Someone's smeared the paint here.

GODFREY
Rosanna or Penelope with their petticoats, no doubt.

FRANKLIN
Petticoats, perhaps… or long robes like those Indian jugglers wore last night.

LADY JULIA
Oh, dear. Is there is no help for it? Must I send for the police?

FRANKLIN
At the very least, the Indians should be taken into custody. I'll ride at once to the magistrate's.

(FRANKLIN exits and GODFREY follows)

LADY JULIA
But how could the Indians have gotten into the house?

BETTEREDGE
(To the audience) With Master Franklin gone, Mr.

Godfrey led the search, but there was no sign of the missing stone. Meanwhile, Rachel remained locked in her chamber, my lady was at her wit's end, and the servants whispered in corners. The cursed Moonstone had turned us all upside down.

(FRANKLIN enters)

LADY JULIA
The Indians? Have they been captured?

FRANKLIN
The poor fellows have been detained for questioning, but they are as innocent as babes. All three were seen in Frizinghall after midnight.

BETTEREDGE
Meaning they walked straight back after their appearance here.

FRANKLIN
Indeed. I took the liberty of sending a telegram to my father; he knows the Chief Commissioner of Police in London, and can lay his hand on the best man to set this to rights.

(GODFREY enters)

GODFREY
Well, I've personally looked over the entire premises and it's clear that no one broke in from the outside.

FRANKLIN
So, the robbery must have been committed by someone in the house.

LADY JULIA
Franklin, you don't mean to accuse one of the

servants—

GODFREY
Nobody's accusing anyone, Aunt Julia, I'm sure.

FRANKLIN
We really must learn what Rachel knows about all this. *(Knocking at RACHEL's door)* Rachel? May we please have a word with you?

RACHEL
(From behind the door) Go away! I have nothing to say to you!

FRANKLIN
What kind of answer is that?

GODFREY
Franklin, go easy on the poor dear. She's suffered quite a shock.

FRANKLIN
What about you, Godfrey? Do you know anything to throw light on this matter?

GODFREY
Me? I'm quite in the dark, I assure you.

FRANKLIN
Your room is right next door.

GODFREY
And yours is just down the hall.

FRANKLIN
You didn't hear any suspicious noises during the night?

GODFREY
Once I got to bed, I slept quite soundly. How did

you sleep?

FRANKLIN
Quite well, actually. What are you implying?

LADY JULIA
Franklin! Godfrey! We mustn't let this set us at each other's throats.

FRANKLIN
Yes, save it for the police, why don't you?

(RACHEL enters from her bedroom)

RACHEL
You summoned the police? *(Pulling FRANKLIN aside)* Why on earth would you do that?

FRANKLIN
We've exhausted every alternative—

RACHEL
What if it were simply misplaced? You haven't searched the entire house yet, surely?

LADY JULIA
Rachel, I know you're upset—

RACHEL
May I please have a moment's privacy? *(To FRANKLIN)* Don't do this.

FRANKLIN
All I'm trying to do is recover your diamond—

RACHEL
This is a vile farce, and I will not be a part of it! *(She storms back to her bedroom)*

GODFREY
Now, Rachel, please…

RACHEL
(Wild and angry) I have not asked for you! I don't want you! My diamond is lost and nobody will ever find it! *(She exits into her bedroom and locks the door)*

BETTEREDGE
(To the audience) I'd never seen the family acting this way before. Suspicion was beginning to tear them apart. And they weren't the only ones behaving strangely. Later, I was passing the library…

(BETTEREDGE passes the library door and notices ROSANNA approaching FRANKLIN, who sits writing at a table. BETTEREDGE watches silently)

ROSANNA
Pardon me, sir…

FRANKLIN
Yes? *(When ROSANNA doesn't respond)* Well, what is it?

ROSANNA
You dropped one of your rings upstairs, Mr. Blake. *(She sets a ring on the table)*

FRANKLIN
(Distracted by his writing) Yes, very good, thank you.

ROSANNA
(Her face flushed, she stares at him intently) Sir, I wanted you to know that they'll never find the person who took the diamond, and I'll answer for that!

BETTEREDGE
(Stepping into the room) Rosanna, what are you doing here? Back to work, girl.

(ROSANNA hurries off)

FRANKLIN
What on earth was that all about?

BETTEREDGE
Oh, sir; if there's somebody ill in the house, trust the women servants for prophesying that the person will die. If a jewel's lost, trust them for saying it will never be found again.

FRANKLIN
As you say, Betteredge. *(He exits)*

BETTEREDGE
(To the audience) Rosanna was later confined to her quarters following an hysterical attack, which Penelope attributed to excess of love for Mr. Franklin. That day wore on to its end quite miserably, I tell you. I hadn't heart enough to open my Robinson Crusoe. The following morning, news came from town by way of Mr. Franklin.

(FRANKLIN enters to join BETTEREDGE)

FRANKLIN
Item the first: the baker's man says he saw Rosanna Spearman yesterday afternoon, walking towards town on the foot path over the moor.

BETTEREDGE
But Rosanna was, all afternoon, ill upstairs in her room.

FRANKLIN
Was she, now? Item the second: the postman says that Dr. Candy caught a chill when he drove off in the rain the other night. He's down with a fever and delirium.

BETTEREDGE
So much for his waterproof skin, eh?

FRANKLIN
(Producing a telegram) Item the third: capital news! The Commissioner is sending the famous Sergeant Cuff, and his arrival is expected by the morning train. If half the stories I have heard are true, there isn't the equal in England of Sergeant Cuff!

BETTEREDGE
(To the audience) When the time came for the arrival of this renowned character, I went down to the gate to meet him. I could not have been more surprised by what I found.

(CUFF enters quietly and approaches BETTEREDGE)

CUFF
Good day. I am Sergeant Cuff.

BETTEREDGE
Gabriel Betteredge, house-steward.

CUFF
The sea air here is quite refreshing, don't you find? And I've been admiring the grounds. You've got the right exposure here. And that is the proper shape for a rosary. Yes, with walks between the beds. But they oughtn't to be gravel. Tell your gardener: grass walks between the roses; gravel's too hard for them. That's a pretty bed of white and blush roses. They always mix well, eh?

BETTEREDGE
You seem to be fond of roses, Sergeant.

CUFF
Soon, please God, I shall retire from catching thieves,

and try my hand at growing roses. And there will be grass walks between my beds. But let's get to work, shall we?

(They cross to meet LADY JULIA, FRANKLIN, and GODFREY)

LADY JULIA
Welcome, Sergeant. It's a pleasure to meet you.

CUFF
No, Lady Julia, the pleasure is mine. Now, I'm sure this affair has caused you no end of discomfort. I'll wish to look about the property and to inspect the sitting room. All this may be done without intruding upon your time any further.

LADY JULIA
My thanks, Sergeant.

CUFF
Oh, and ma'am...?

LADY JULIA
Yes?

CUFF
Might I urge your ladyship to employ her gardener to try grass? No gravel!

(LADY JULIA exits; the others cross to the sitting room. CUFF discovers the smeared paint)

CUFF
That's a pity. How did it happen?

GODFREY
Oh, you know; one of the women and their petticoats in all the confusion yesterday morning, Sergeant. A trifle, a mere trifle.

CUFF
I made an investigation recently; at one end of which there was a murder, and at the other was a spot of ink that nobody could account for. In my experience along the dirtiest ways of this dirty little world, I never met with such a thing as a trifle yet. Before we go any further, we must see the petticoat that made the smear, and we must know for certain when that paint was wet.

FRANKLIN
That door, Sergeant, was painted by Miss Verinder, with a vehicle of my own composition, which dries in twelve hours.

CUFF
And do you remember when this portion was completed, sir?

FRANKLIN
Three o'clock on the afternoon of Rachel's birthday.

CUFF
And the vehicle dried it in twelve hours; that is to say, by three in the morning... *(To GODFREY)* long before the time you supposed that the servants' petticoats smeared it. *(To FRANKLIN)* It's quite possible, sir, that you have put the clue into our hands.

RACHEL
(Entering from her bedroom) You, there. Did you say that he put the clue into your hands?

CUFF
He has possibly given us a clue. Having answered your question, miss, may I make an inquiry of my own? There is a smear on the painting of your door.

Do you know when it was done?

RACHEL
Are you the police officer?

CUFF
I am Sergeant Cuff, miss, of the Detective Police.

RACHEL
Do you think a lady's advice worth having?

CUFF
I shall be glad to hear it.

RACHEL
Do your duty yourself, and don't allow Franklin Blake to help you! *(She exits to her bedroom)*

CUFF
Miss Verinder appears to be a little out of temper about the loss of her diamond. Natural enough! Well, we know when the paint was dry. The next thing to discover is when the paint was last seen without that smear. You've got a head about you; you must understand what I mean.

BETTEREDGE
The more we narrow the question of time, the more we narrow the field of inquiry.

CUFF
Correct, sir. Who was the last person in the room on the birthday night?

BETTEREDGE
My daughter Penelope, sir. She is Miss Verinder's maid. I'll ask her to step up.

CUFF
Wait. We must tread carefully. Tell your daughter,

and the other servants, I have no evidence that the diamond was stolen; I only know it is lost. All I want is their help in finding it.

BETTEREDGE
(To the audience) That smoothed them down, from the cook to the scullion, to be sure.

(PENELOPE enters)

PENELOPE
When I wished Miss Rachel good night at midnight, I used the handle on the door, and, knowing the paint was wet, took pains not to touch it. There was no smear then.

CUFF
Could you swear that your dress mightn't have touched it accidentally?

PENELOPE
Yes. I remember the dress I had on and there's not the ghost of a stain on it.

CUFF
Good girl. I'll want to examine that dress at your earliest convenience. You may go.

(PENELOPE exits)

CUFF
So, somebody must have been in the room between midnight and three o'clock. There are now some discoveries to make. Find out, first, the article of dress with a smear of paint on it. Find out, second, who it belongs to. Find that out, and you haven't far to look for the hand that has got the diamond. *(To GODFREY)* This trifle of yours has grown in importance.

GODFREY
There is such a thing, Sergeant, as making a mountain out of a molehill.

CUFF
There is also such a thing as making nothing out of a molehill. Mr. Betteredge, I require a moment with your mistress.

FRANKLIN
Wait, Sergeant. Do you already have a guess as to who has stolen the diamond?

CUFF
Nobody has stolen the diamond.

GODFREY
What on earth do you mean?

CUFF
Wait a little. The pieces of the puzzle are not all put together yet.

(They cross to meet LADY JULIA in her sitting room)

LADY JULIA
And how do you propose to discover the article of dress with the smear of paint upon it?

CUFF
I must beg your ladyship's permission to search the servants' rooms.

LADY JULIA
I will not permit my good servants to be insulted in that way!

CUFF
What if I were to examine the wardrobes of every-

body – from your ladyship downwards – who slept in the house on Wednesday night? It would be a mere formality, of course, but the servants would accept it as even dealing between themselves and their betters.

LADY JULIA
Very well. *(To BETTEREDGE)* You will speak to them, Gabriel.

CUFF
Wait. Hadn't we better ensure first that the other ladies and gentlemen will consent, as well?

LADY JULIA
The only other lady in the house is Miss Verinder. The only gentlemen are my nephews. There is not the least fear of refusal from any of the three. Though, I believe Godfrey must return to town this morning...

GODFREY
Rest assured that I would never stand in the way of the investigation. *(He hands a luggage key to CUFF)* My luggage can follow me to London, when the inquiry is over. Thank you again, Aunt Julia, for your hospitality. And tell Rachel I have not taken No for an answer.

FRANKLIN
(To GODFREY) I'll take you to the station. *(To CUFF)* All my belongings are open to examination. Nothing I possess is kept under lock and key.

(GODFREY and FRANKLIN exit)

CUFF
Before we obtain Miss Rachel's blessing, with your

ladyship's permission I should like to have the washing book. The stained article of dress may be an article of linen. If the search leads to nothing, I want to be able to account for all the linen sent to the wash.

BETTEREDGE
(To the audience) We sent for the washing book at once.

(ROSANNA enters with the washing book. She hands it miserably to CUFF and then exits)

CUFF
How long has that woman been in your employment?

LADY JULIA
Why do you ask?

CUFF
Because the last time I saw her she was in prison for theft.

BETTEREDGE
(To the audience) There was no help for it, but to tell him the truth about Rosanna's history. Then we went to Miss Rachel with my lady's instructions that she turn over her keys.

(BETTEREDGE and CUFF cross to RACHEL's sitting room. RACHEL responds from behind her door)

RACHEL
I refuse to have my belongings examined!

CUFF
(In the tone of a man who hears something he'd expected to hear) Ah! Well, we must examine all the wardrobes in the house or none. Send Mr. Ablewhite's luggage

to London by the next train, and return the washing book, with my compliments, to the young woman who brought it in.

BETTEREDGE
You don't seem to be much disappointed.

CUFF
Come take a walk with me, Mr. Betteredge. Let's have a look at the garden.

(They cross to the garden, CUFF whistling The Last Rose of Summer. ROSANNA enters separately, and spies on them from behind the shrubbery)

BETTEREDGE
You're welcome to take a rose, if you wish to, Sergeant.

CUFF
No, but thank you. It hurts my heart to break them off the stem. Now, you are an observant man; did you notice anything strange in any of the servants, making allowance, of course, for fright and fluster, after the theft was found out? Anyone not in their usual spirits? Unexpectedly taken ill?

BETTEREDGE
We all lost our heads together, myself included.

CUFF
And that's all you have to tell me, is it?

(BETTEREDGE is deciding whether or not to mention ROSANNA when CUFF spies her in her hiding place. CUFF groans audibly and rubs his back)

BETTEREDGE
What's the matter?

CUFF
(Loudly enough for ROSANNA to hear) A touch of the rheumatics in my back. We shall have a change in the weather before long. Come along, let's keep walking.

(They turn a corner in the garden and CUFF lowers his voice. ROSANNA exits)

CUFF
That Rosanna Spearman? She doesn't have a sweetheart hereabouts, does she?

BETTEREDGE
Why do you ask?

CUFF
I saw her hiding in the shrubbery as we went by.

BETTEREDGE
Ah, what in God's name am I to say to you now?

CUFF
Say what you know; no more, no less.

BETTEREDGE
This is Mr. Franklin's favorite walk; he'll come this way when returning from the station. And if my daughter is right, Rosanna is mad enough to have set her heart on him.

CUFF
Don't worry; I'll keep it a secret. I like to be tender to human infirmity; though I don't get many chances in my line of work.

(CUFF crosses to an interior room, where he is met by PENELOPE. CUFF interrogates her in dumb show)

BETTEREDGE
(To the audience) That afternoon, the Sergeant requested that I send in the servants to see him, one at a time...

(PENELOPE storms out of CUFF's room to join BETTEREDGE as ROSANNA crosses to join CUFF)

PENELOPE
Well, I never! If Sergeant Cuff refuses to believe me, he can...

(PENELOPE exits muttering to herself. ROSANNA is interrogated in dumb show behind the following)

BETTEREDGE
(To the audience) Rosanna remained longer with the Sergeant than any of them.

(ROSANNA exits CUFF's room and passes BETTEREDGE in silence. CUFF crosses to BETTEREDGE)

CUFF
If Rosanna Spearman asks leave to go out again, let the poor thing go; but let me know first. (He exits)

BETTEREDGE
(To the audience) I don't know how he knew to expect it, but word came shortly from the cook that Rosanna did ask to go out for a breath of fresh air. My curiosity being roused, I took it upon me to question Penelope.

(PENELOPE enters)

PENELOPE
I never, for one moment, believed Rosanna's illness.

In fact, I snuck upstairs, several times during the afternoon, and her door was locked. I knocked; no answer! Then I saw a light under her door at midnight. And later I heard the crackling of a fire. In June! At four in the morning! I told this to the Sergeant, but he said I was making it up. I never! *(She exits)*

BETTEREDGE
(To the audience) I walked out into the garden, feeling very uneasy at the turn things had taken. There, I met Master Franklin returning from the station. I told him what had transpired.

(FRANKLIN enters and joins BETTEREDGE)

FRANKLIN
We know that Rosanna was seen yesterday on the way to Frizinghall when we supposed her to be in her room. The paint-stained dress must belong to her; and the fire in her room was lit to destroy it. Rosanna has stolen the diamond. I'll go tell my aunt.

(CUFF enters)

CUFF
Not just yet, if you please.

FRANKLIN
Mr. Cuff, I am to understand that you forbid me to tell my aunt what has happened?

CUFF
You are to understand, sir, that I give up the case if you tell anybody, until I give you leave.

(FRANKLIN storms off. During the following, ROSANNA is seen making her way to a high ledge over

the Shivering Sand. She wraps a length of chain around an old tin box and uses the chain to sink the box in the quicksand, fastening the upper end of the chain to a location not visible from above)

CUFF
Mr. Betteredge, you have done a very foolish thing in my absence. In the future, I hope you will do your detective business along with me. Now, you are determined to give me no information against Rosanna Spearman, because she has been good to you, and you pity her heartily. Those humane considerations do you credit, but you must leave them behind. Surely you know what she was about yesterday? She finds the stain on her nightgown, shams ill and slips away to town to get materials. She makes a new dress last night, lighting a fire to iron the substitute, and is at this moment making away with the stained dress. I followed her just now, leaving the house with an old tin case and a length of chain. She was headed towards the sea, that much I could tell; but I lost her. Do you have a guess as to where she might go? Some place secret, or special to her?

BETTEREDGE
The Shivering Sand.

CUFF
Show me.

(They walk towards the Shivering Sand)

BETTEREDGE
(To the audience) If there is such a thing as detective fever, that disease had got fast hold of me. We went on to the beach, searching high and low, till the last

of the evening light was fading away...

CUFF
Rosanna understands the virtues of sand quite well! She got to and fro, without any marks to trace her by, walking through the water from this point till she got to those rocks.

BETTEREDGE
We'll never pick up her trail now.

CUFF
What the girl has done is clear enough. She fastened the chain to the case and sunk it in the quicksand. And she will leave it hidden till the present proceedings are over. But the mystery is: what the devil has she hidden in the case?

BETTEREDGE
Can't you guess?

CUFF
It's not the diamond. The whole experience of my life is at fault, if it is.

BETTEREDGE
The stained dress!

CUFF
But why not simply tie up a stone in the dress and throw it into the quicksand? Why hide it? None of this makes sense! Excuse my being out of temper; I have let Rosanna Spearman puzzle me.

(BETTEREDGE and CUFF cross to the Verinder house, where they catch sight of ROSANNA approaching FRANKLIN exiting his bedroom. BETTEREDGE is about to speak, but CUFF silences him. ROSANNA touches FRANKLIN's arm)

FRANKLIN
Ah, you startled me. *(He steps away as ROSANNA simply stares at him like a ghost)* Did you wish to speak to me?

ROSANNA
Yes, if I dare... *(She attempts to summon her courage, but remains silent)*

FRANKLIN
Well...? *(He grows uncomfortable and cannot maintain eye contact with her)*

ROSANNA
He looks at anything else rather than look at me!

(ROSANNA flees, turning a corner and collapsing out of sight, but not out of hearing of the next scene. BETTEREDGE and CUFF step forward to join FRANKLIN)

FRANKLIN
Did you see that? I didn't know what to say to the poor thing. I've been too hard on her, perhaps, in my thoughts...

CUFF
Have you now?

FRANKLIN
Is there something you wish to say to me?

CUFF
You needn't be afraid of harming the girl, sir. On the contrary, I recommend you to honor me with your confidence, if you feel any interest in Rosanna Spearman.

FRANKLIN

I take no interest whatever in Rosanna Spearman. I never have, and I never will.

(With a cry that catches their attention, ROSANNA exits entirely)

BETTEREDGE
Prying, and peeping, and listening; in another day or two, we shall all be struck down. I wish to God that diamond had never found its way into this house.

(FRANKLIN and CUFF exit)

BETTEREDGE
(To the audience) That night, I confess, I felt wretchedly worn out, and unfit for my place, and began to wonder, for the first time, when it would please God to take me. In the morning, the Sergeant went to Frizinghall, while I sought out Rosanna.

(BETTEREDGE discovers ROSANNA listlessly about her work)

BETTEREDGE
Come now; cheer up, Rosanna. Mr. Franklin feels terrible about his behavior—

ROSANNA
(As if in a dream) Mr. Franklin is very kind and considerate. Thank you.

BETTEREDGE
Now, now, my girl! This is not like you. You have something on your mind. Don't keep it in any longer. I'll stand your friend, even if you have done wrong. Make an end to this, Rosanna!

ROSANNA
Yes. I'll make an end of it.

BETTEREDGE
Very good. Let's go speak to my lady.

ROSANNA
No. I'll come clean to Mr. Franklin when I finish my work. Thank you, Mr. Betteredge. *(She exits)*

BETTEREDGE
(To the audience) It was over an hour before Sergeant Cuff returned.

(CUFF enters. During the following, ROSANNA races to the Shivering Sand. She reaches a high ledge and stares out over the deeps)

CUFF
The Indians have been released. They have nothing to do with the loss of the jewel. But I was able to verify what Rosanna bought in Frizinghall the other day: enough long cloth to make a nightgown.

BETTEREDGE
Whose?

CUFF
Her own, to be sure; plain long cloth means a servant's nightgown. The pinch still is: why, after providing the substitute dress, does she hide the smeared nightgown, instead of destroying it? If the girl won't speak out, there is only one way of settling this: I must see Miss Verinder.

BETTEREDGE
Miss Verinder? *(Grabbing CUFF by the lapels)* Damn you! There's something wrong with Rachel and you have been hiding it from me all this time! *(Releasing him)* I beg your pardon, sir. Please remember, that I have served this family for years. Rachel climbed

upon my knees as a child.

CUFF
Don't distress yourself, Mr. Betteredge. If it's any comfort to you, collar me again. You don't know how to do it; but I'll overlook your awkwardness in consideration of your feelings.

BETTEREDGE
Tell me the truth. What do you suspect?

CUFF
I don't suspect. I know. Miss Verinder has been in secret possession of the Moonstone from first to last; and she has taken Rosanna Spearman into her confidence. There is the case in a nutshell.

BETTEREDGE
But why on earth would she steal her own diamond?

(PENELOPE enters)

PENELOPE
Begging your pardon, father, but cook says that Rosanna has disappeared again. No one can account for her.

BETTEREDGE
When was she last seen?

PENELOPE
About an hour ago. She went through the kitchen with a letter, and asked the butcher's man to post it for her.

CUFF
And she hasn't been seen since?

PENELOPE
No, sir. *(She exits)*

BETTEREDGE
The location of the hiding place must be in that letter!

CUFF
For certain. But first, we must find Rosanna Spearman.

(CUFF and BETTEREDGE head to the Shivering Sand. The sky darkens and thunder booms in the distance. Meanwhile, at the Sands, ROSANNA hurls herself off the ledge and into the quicksand, where she sinks into the deeps)

CUFF
(Shouting above the elements to BETTEREDGE) Come on! We're losing the light! Wait! Here! A footprint in the sand, bearing straight towards that rocky ledge. Oh, no...

(BETTEREDGE and CUFF scramble up the ledge and stare out over the quicksand)

BETTEREDGE
(To the audience) In all directions, quicksand, sea, and storm. No sign of life.

CUFF
She tried to reach her hiding place. But some fatal accident happened to her on these rocks.

BETTEREDGE
There was no accident. When she came to this place, she came weary of her life. The deeps of the quicksand have got her. And what the Sand gets, the Sand keeps forever.
(BETTEREDGE collapses into tears. CUFF attempts to lay a comforting hand on his shoulder)

BETTEREDGE
Don't you touch me! It's the dread of you that drove her to this.

CUFF
Come now, Mr. Betteredge. Let's go back.

BETTEREDGE
We can't go back now. A life has been lost. There's no returning; not anymore.

(At the house, they encounter LADY JULIA and RACHEL heading for the front door, followed by PENELOPE, who carries RACHEL's luggage. FRANKLIN enters the hall from another door)

LADY JULIA
My dear, please wait...

RACHEL
I've made up my mind.

FRANKLIN
What's going on here?

LADY JULIA
Rachel is leaving. She wishes to stay at our home in London.

CUFF
Is there a reason for your sudden departure, miss?

RACHEL
I can no longer bear the presence of a policeman under the same roof. *(To LADY JULIA, kissing her on the cheeks)* Try to forgive me.

CUFF
Wait, miss. I can't stop you from traveling to London.

I can only say that your leaving puts an obstacle in the way of recovering your diamond. Knowing that, do you still choose to depart?

RACHEL
Goodbye, mamma. *(She starts to exit)*

CUFF
(Stopping RACHEL in her tracks) Miss Verinder, Rosanna Spearman is dead.

RACHEL
What?

LADY JULIA
(To BETTEREDGE) Gabriel, is this true?

BETTEREDGE
I'm so sorry, my lady. She's gone.

LADY JULIA
Give that wretch his money and release me from the sight of him!

CUFF
My lady; we must face this distressing calamity. Some unbearable anxiety over the diamond drove Rosanna to her own destruction. Now, I don't know what that anxiety was, but I think, with your permission, I can lay my hand on the person who does.

LADY JULIA
You suspect my daughter of stealing her own diamond? Is that true?

CUFF
Quite true, my lady.

LADY JULIA
Your knowledge of her character dates from a day

or two since. My knowledge of her dates from the beginning of her life.

CUFF
Young ladies often have private debts which they daren't acknowledge, sometimes for purposes which I won't shock you by mentioning. Bear this in mind, and look at recent events. Miss Verinder betrays an illogical resentment against everyone who has tried to recover her lost jewel. She declines to be questioned. When I suggest examining her wardrobe, she refuses point–blank. If she is not privy to the suppression of the diamond, what do these things mean?

LADY JULIA
I suspect you're about to tell us, Sergeant.

CUFF
I wondered: would Miss Verinder be satisfied with leading us all to believe the Moonstone was merely lost? Or would she go a step further, and make us think it had been stolen? Enter Rosanna Spearman, a former thief; the perfect person to lead us off on a false scent.

LADY JULIA
No, she left that life behind her.

CUFF
You cannot escape your past. Who else could help Miss Verinder sell the diamond? No young lady in her position could manage such a risky matter by herself. She must have a go–between, and who so fit as Rosanna? She had relations with one of the few money lenders in London who would handle such a notable jewel. Now, I'm sorry to spring this

on you in this way, but it was my hope that a great shock might hurry Miss Verinder's better feelings into making a clean breast of it.

RACHEL
You hear me, Sergeant, for I will only say this once. I owe no money to any living creature. I never spoke a word in private to Rosanna. And the diamond has not been in my possession since my birthday.

CUFF
With all respect, miss; the evidence suggests otherwise.

RACHEL
The day will come when you will know why I am silent... *(To LADY JULIA)* even to you. I have done much to make my mother pity me, but nothing to make her ashamed of me.

LADY JULIA
Sergeant, in resigning all further claim on your services, I have only to say that while I would like to believe in your honesty and intelligence, I am firmly persuaded that the circumstances, in this case, have fatally misled you.

(LADY JULIA and RACHEL start to exit but FRANKLIN steps forward)

FRANKLIN
Rachel, please. Don't go.

(Without a word, RACHEL exits. LADY JULIA follows)

CUFF
We aren't done with the Moonstone yet. Allow

me to turn prophet. I believe three things will happen in the future, whether you like it or not. First, you will hear of it when the postman delivers Rosanna's letter. Second, you will hear of the three Indians again.

BETTEREDGE
And the third?

CUFF
You will hear of that money lender in London, whom I just mentioned. I'll even verify his name: Mr. Septimus Luker. Time will show whether I am right or wrong. In the meanwhile, sir, I carry away with me a sincere personal liking for you, which I think does honor to us both. If we don't meet again before my retirement, I hope you will come and see me in the little house which I have got my eye on. There will be grass walks, I promise you, in my garden. *(He exits)*

FRANKLIN
How do you explain Rachel's conduct, Betteredge?

BETTEREDGE
Perhaps, sir, we should consult Robinson Crusoe for advice.

FRANKLIN
What do we know? The loss of the Moonstone has thrown her into a state of anxiety. Being in this state, Rachel, properly speaking, is not Rachel, but Somebody Else. Do I mind being cruelly treated by Somebody Else? Of course not. But how does it end?

BETTEREDGE
It ends, I dare say, with me retiring to my room to

find solace in the most composing pipe of tobacco I will ever smoke in my life.

FRANKLIN
(Pulling out his cigar case) Can I have smoked as long as I have without discovering that the answer for dealing with women is at the bottom of my cigar case? Follow me here: you choose a cigar, you try it, and it disappoints you. What do you do? Fool! You throw it away and try another!

BETTEREDGE
When the late Mrs. Betteredge was alive, I felt often inclined to try your philosophy. But the law insists on your smoking your cigar, sir, when once you have chosen it.

FRANKLIN
Goodbye, Betteredge. There's nothing left for me here. Please send my luggage after me.

BETTEREDGE
You're not going to leave us, sir?

FRANKLIN
I should never have brought that stone into this house. When I came here, there wasn't a happier household in England. Look at us now! Scattered, disunited, the very air of the place poisoned with suspicion. The Moonstone has served the Colonel's vengeance better than he ever dreamt of! *(He exits)*

(PENELOPE enters and joins BETTEREDGE)

BETTEREDGE
(To the audience) Well, I shall soon have done with my part of the story, and shall hand over the reins to the person following me. If you are as tired of

hearing me speak as I am of talking — Lord, how we shall all enjoy ourselves a few minutes further on! My lady and Miss Rachel moved directly on to London. Most of the servants went with them, including Penelope. I was left in the country, to mourn Rosanna, alone.

PENELOPE
(To the audience) When we got to London, we found that rumor followed us. The city was soon buzzing with gossip about Miss Rachel and the Sergeant's suspicion of her guilt. Doors were closed to her; letters returned unopened. She and my lady were cast out of society.

BETTEREDGE
(To the audience) A scattered and disunited household, indeed. On Monday, the first of Sergeant Cuff's prophecies came true. *(He displays a letter)* The letter sent by Rosanna arrived, addressed to Mr. Franklin. I sent word, but the young master had already left for foreign parts. To where, nobody knew. What the letter contained, we would not know till he returned. Then, a few days later, the post brought me a letter from Sergeant Cuff containing a clipping from a London newspaper.

(CUFF and LUKER appear)

CUFF
Yesterday, Mr. Septimus Luker, well-known dealer in ancient gems, applied to the magistrate...

LUKER
I was annoyed, at several intervals during the day, by three of those strolling Indians who infest our streets. After being sent away by the police, they

returned, entering my house on pretence of seeking charity. It is my belief that a robbery is contemplated. Only yesterday, I was compelled to dismiss a foreign workman in my service on suspicion of theft. Something must be done! *(He exits)*

BETTEREDGE

(To the audience) There it was: the accomplishment of Sergeant Cuff's three predictions in less than a week! It seemed that Miss Rachel had gone to Mr. Luker, and that the Moonstone was in pledge in the moneylender's house. Well, in the dark, I have brought you thus far. In the dark I am compelled to leave you now, with my best respects. May you find in my words what Robinson Crusoe found in his experience on the desert island, namely, "something to comfort yourselves from."

BLACKOUT

END OF ACT ONE

ACT II

(Lights rise on FRANKLIN and CLACK)

FRANKLIN
(To the audience) So, the devil's dance of the Indian diamond has threaded its way to London; and to London we go after it. We turn now to Rachel's cousin, Miss Clack. *(He exits)*

CLACK
(To the audience) I am indebted to my dear parents – both now in heaven – for having instilled in me, at a very early age, the strictest habits of order, regularity, and keen observation: my hair is always tidy, and my eyes opened wide. After my parents' passing, I sought the solace of a solitary life in service to God, wanting nothing to do with the Herncastles and their deplorable scandals. But you cannot hide from your own family. You cannot escape the past. Despite my reservations, I will share all that I witnessed in this unfortunate case.

No doubt, Mr. Blake will wish to contradict what may not prove to be sufficiently flattering to the person chiefly involved—

(FRANKLIN enters)

FRANKLIN
Miss Clack, rest assured that nothing will be contradicted. Whatever opinions you may express, not a word will be argued with, from first to last. *(He exits)*

CLACK
We shall see. *(To the audience)* This all began when I visited Aunt Verinder's London home in July of 1848. I am normally ignorant of secular goings-on, yet I couldn't help but hear the rumors that traveled to London with my aunt and her daughter – I shudder to call her my cousin! I thought they might find comfort in the company of a friend who would not pass judgment upon them.

(CLACK stops at the door of LADY JULIA's London estate. PENELOPE answers the door)

CLACK
(To the audience) The door was answered by the daughter of that heathen old man Betteredge.

PENELOPE
Lady Julia would be delighted to have you for tea.

CLACK
Having always a few helpful religious writings on hand, I selected one applicable to her, on the sinfulness of dress, titled, "A Word With You On Your Cap-Ribbons."

(CLACK hands PENELOPE the tract and crosses into the sitting room to join LADY JULIA and RACHEL)

PENELOPE
Well, I never…

(PENELOPE serves tea while RACHEL, feverishly excited, pores through newspapers littered about the room)

CLACK
(To the audience) Dear Aunt Verinder received me with her usual grace and kindness, but I never saw Rachel without wondering how a person like that could be the child of such a distinguished mother. *(To LADY JULIA)* We had a meeting last night of the Select Committee of the Mothers'–Small–Clothes–Conversion–Society. The object of this excellent charity, you must know, is to rescue unredeemed fathers' trousers from the pawnbroker and prevent their resumption, on the part of the irreclaimable parent, by abridging them immediately to fit the innocent son.

RACHEL
Yes, we know all about your Conversion Club…

CLACK
I mention the Society, because our dear friend, Mr. Godfrey Ablewhite, was expected, but to my great disappointment he never appeared.

RACHEL
Oh, Clack, have you not heard the news? It's in all the papers.

CLACK
What news?

LADY JULIA

Godfrey and another gentlemen—

RACHEL
Septimus Luker.

LADY JULIA
—were the victims of an outrage the other day.

CLACK
What happened?

(GODFREY, LUKER, and the INDIANS enact the events as RACHEL recounts the tale, pulling information from multiple newspapers)

RACHEL
Godfrey was cashing a cheque at a bank in Lombard Street. On departing, he ran into a perfect stranger who was leaving the office at the same time. They said a few civil words, bowed, and parted.

CLACK
(To the audience) You may say, "Here is an incident unrelated to the subject at hand." My fellow sinners, beware of relying upon your poor carnal reason. Let your faith be as your stockings, and your stockings as your faith. Both ever spotless, and both ready to put on at a moment's notice! Let me mention that the stranger was Mr. Luker, and resume our story.

RACHEL
Returning home, Godfrey found a letter requesting his attendance in Northumberland Street, with the promise of a donation to one of his Societies by an elderly lady of ill health.

CLACK
And, of course, the Christian Hero never hesitates where good is to be done.

RACHEL
Godfrey went to the house. He was directed to an apartment at the back, when suddenly…

(GODFREY is surprised by INDIAN #1, who seizes him round the neck from behind. INDIANS #2 and #3 join in and GODFREY is pulled to the floor, bound, his eyes covered, and his mouth gagged. The INDIANS search him, but do not discover what they seek)

RACHEL
Later that same day, Luker received a letter from a collector of Oriental antiquities, summoning him to a home in Alfred Place. He went to meet his new patron and the exact thing that happened to Godfrey happened to Mr. Luker!

(LUKER is seized by the INDIANS in same manner as GODFREY)

RACHEL
The only difference was when Mr. Luker's pockets were turned out; a paper he carried was taken, acknowledging the receipt of a valuable which Mr. Luker had left in the strong room of the bank. But the document is useless for fraud, as the item can only be given up to Luker himself.

CLACK
Have the police been able to shed any light on these attacks?

RACHEL
They believe that a robbery was planned on bad information. The thieves were plainly unsure if Mr. Luker carried his precious object or not.

LADY JULIA
And poor Godfrey paid the penalty of being seen accidentally speaking to him. Now, come, Rachel; do sit down. Remember what the doctor said about quieting yourself.

RACHEL
I'll go to the library, mamma. But if Godfrey calls, mind I am told of it. I am dying to see him. *(She kisses her mother on the cheek and then passes CLACK brusquely)* Clack. *(She exits)*

CLACK
(To the audience) I made a private memorandum to pray for her. When we were alone, my aunt told me the whole horrible story of the Indian diamond.

LADY JULIA
The doctors recommend rest for Rachel, and urge me to keep her from dwelling on the past. I do my best, but this strange adventure of Godfrey's happens at a most unfortunate time.

CLACK
Your knowledge of the world, dear aunt, is superior to mine, but it is obvious to me that she is keeping a sinful secret from you.

LADY JULIA
Rachel assures me she has done nothing wrong, and I choose to believe her.

(GODFREY enters like a tragic hero and both ladies rise to fuss over him)

GODFREY
Aunt Julia! And Miss Clack!

LADY JULIA
Oh, dear Godfrey, tell me you're all right!

CLACK
Yes, Mr. Ablewhite, do you feel like yourself again?

GODFREY
Ah, ladies, what have I done to deserve all this sympathy? I have merely been mistaken for somebody else, blindfolded, strangled, and thrown onto a very hard floor. Just think how much worse it might have been! I might have been murdered or robbed. But what have I lost? Nothing at all. If I could have my way, I would have kept my adventure to myself; I shrink from all this fuss and publicity.

LADY JULIA
This shall all pass soon enough, Godfrey.

GODFREY
And Miss Clack, I am sadly behind with my Committee work and my dear Ladies. Did you make progress at the meeting? Are we nicely off for Trousers?

(RACHEL reenters, rushing directly to GODFREY)

RACHEL
Godfrey! I'm so glad to see you! Tell me what the papers left out.

GODFREY
Dearest Rachel, the newspapers have told you everything, and much better than I can.

LADY JULIA
Godfrey thinks we all make too much of the matter.

CLACK
True greatness is ever modest.

RACHEL
My dear Godfrey, you live too much in the society of women and have contracted two very bad habits in consequence. You talk nonsense seriously, and you tell fibs for the pleasure of telling them. Come, I am brimful of questions. Are the men who captured you the Indians who visited us in the country?

GODFREY
I cannot say. They blindfolded me before I could see their faces.

RACHEL
Tell me about Mr. Luker.

GODFREY
I know nothing of Mr. Luker. I never saw him before we met accidentally at the bank.

RACHEL
The receipt they took; what was it for?

GODFREY
Some valuable deposited by Mr. Luker. That is all I know.

LADY JULIA
Surely the police can make him reveal more than that.

GODFREY
Believe me, they tried. But Luker won't say a word, out of respect for his client's privacy.

RACHEL
Tell me plainly, Godfrey, do you believe that Luker had the Moonstone?

GODFREY
He solemnly declares that, before this scandal, he never even heard of the Moonstone. Yet all the rumormongers insist, without proof, that he's hiding something. Shameful!

RACHEL
Considering you don't know Mr. Luker, you take up his cause rather warmly.

GODFREY
I hope, Rachel, I take up the cause of all oppressed people rather warmly.

RACHEL
Keep your noble sentiments for your Ladies, Godfrey. Why are you so unwilling to speak? What does scandal say of you?

GODFREY
(Reluctantly) That the Moonstone is pledged to Mr. Luker, and I'm the man who pawned it.

LADY JULIA
(Rising to her feet) Godfrey!

(The others rise as well and RACHEL crosses to GODFREY. LADY JULIA misses a step, suddenly very weak. CLACK is the only one who notices, but LADY JULIA waves her to be silent)

RACHEL
Oh, God; this is all my fault! I can't bear it! I had a right to sacrifice myself, but to let an innocent man be ruined... I must put a stop to this!

GODFREY
Rachel, really, this will be forgotten in another week.

RACHEL
All of you, hear what I say! I know for a fact that Godfrey Ablewhite is innocent. Take me to the magistrate, and I will swear it!

GODFREY
You must not appear publicly in such a thing as this.

RACHEL
I cannot allow you to be disgraced; if you won't take me to the magistrate, draw out a declaration of your innocence on paper, and I will sign it. Do it, or I'll go out and cry it in the streets!

GODFREY
I will do so, on condition that we never speak of this again.

RACHEL
Let's go prepare your paper. *(To LADY JULIA)* I have not distressed you, have I, mamma?

LADY JULIA
No, no, my dear. Go; do what you have to do.

(RACHEL breaks down in tears)

CLACK
Poor Rachel. A heavy heart is one of the greatest torments the Almighty can lay upon a guilty conscience.

RACHEL
Don't you pity me, Clack. Come on, Godfrey. *(She exits with GODFREY)*

CLACK
Are you all right, Aunt Julia?

LADY JULIA
(Pointing to a nearby phial) Quick! Six drops, in water.

(CLACK gives the medicine to LADY JULIA. She drinks it, and steadies herself against the back of a chair)

LADY JULIA
Drusilla, you have surprised a secret which I had confided to my lawyer, Mr. Bruff, and no one else. Can I trust in your discretion?

CLACK
I am entirely at your disposal.

LADY JULIA
Keep me company, then, this afternoon, till Mr. Bruff arrives. And you can be my witness when I sign my Will.

CLACK
Your Will?

LADY JULIA
I have been seriously ill for some time, without knowing it. When I brought Rachel to London for medical advice, one of the doctors discovered that I suffer from an insidious form of heart disease, which has fatally broken me down. I may die before another day has passed; so I am doing my best to set my worldly affairs in order. But Rachel must be kept in the dark. If she knew, she would attribute my broken health to anxiety over the diamond, and would blame herself bitterly. I trust you will keep my secret, Drusilla, for I believe I see sincere sympathy in your face.

CLACK
Oh, the good I mean to do you, before we part!

(Drawing forth a collection of tracts) I possess a small library of tracts, all suitable to the present emergency. You will read them, won't you?

LADY JULIA
(Setting the tracts aside in distaste) I will do what I can, Drusilla, to please you.

(GODFREY enters with a paper)

GODFREY
Well, here it is: Rachel's statement of my innocence. I hope that you will both bear witness that I destroyed it before I left the house? *(He lights a match and burns the paper)* Any inconvenience I may suffer is nothing compared with preserving Rachel's good name.

LADY JULIA
You are a better man than she may ever know, Godfrey. We are blessed to have you.

GODFREY
No, Aunt Julia; it is I who am blessed. Good day.

(GODFREY exits as BRUFF enters. The signing of the Will is enacted in dumb show behind the following)

CLACK
(To the audience) When the lawyer arrived, I witnessed the signing of Lady Verinder's Will. It was rather hurried over, to my thinking, in indecent haste by Mr. Bruff.

BRUFF
(To the audience) It was handled entirely properly, I assure you.

LADY JULIA

I hope you won't think yourself neglected, Drusilla. I mean to give you your little legacy with my own hand.

CLACK
(Drawing forth a tract and handing it to LADY JULIA) Give your attention, dear aunt, to this precious text, and you will give me all I ask.

LADY JULIA
(Perusing the tract) "The Serpent at Home."

CLACK
The chapters best suited to female perusal are "Satan in the Hair Brush," "Satan behind the Looking Glass," and "Satan under the Tea Table."

LADY JULIA
(Returning the tract) I fear I must wait till I am a little better. I should rest now. *(She exits)*

CLACK
(Slipping the tract under a sofa cushion) I will call again tomorrow!

(During the following conversation, CLACK slips tracts into clever hiding places all around the room)

BRUFF
Well, Miss Clack, what's the latest news in the charitable circles? How is your friend Mr. Ablewhite? Egad! They're telling pretty stores about him at my club!

CLACK
Any scandalous stories told of him are vile falsehoods.

BRUFF

Appearances are dead against him: in the house when the diamond was lost; first person to go to London afterwards. Ugly circumstances, ma'am.

CLACK
I don't presume to argue with a clever lawyer like you, but remember that the famous Sergeant Cuff put suspicion on Rachel.

BRUFF
And you believe him?

CLACK
I judge nobody, sir, and offer no opinion.

BRUFF
Bah! The Sergeant was utterly wrong. If he knew Rachel as I do, he would have suspected everybody in the house but her.

CLACK
Permit me to inform you that the innocence of Mr. Ablewhite was just proclaimed by Rachel herself. What do you say to that?

BRUFF
If she has testified to his innocence, then I have been misled, like the rest of the world.

CLACK
You mentioned, as one of the reasons for suspecting Mr. Ablewhite, that he was in the house when the diamond was lost. Let me remind you that Franklin Blake was also in the house.

BRUFF
Careful, Miss Clack. Franklin Blake is a favorite of mine. But, for the sake of argument, let's adopt your view and suspect him. It's quite in his char-

acter, one might say, to be capable of stealing the Moonstone. But was it in his interest to do so?

CLACK
Mr. Blake's debts are matters of family notoriety.

BRUFF
I manage his affairs, you should know, and his creditors are quite content to charge interest, and wait for their money. Besides, Rachel was ready to marry him, before that infernal diamond disappeared. So there he was: his creditors appeased, and soon to be wedded to an heiress. He had no motive. Why the devil he should steal the Moonstone?

CLACK
Mr. Bruff! If I hear the devil referred to, I must leave the room!

BRUFF
I beg your pardon, Miss Clack. I'll be more careful with my choice of language in the future.

CLACK
(To the audience) Despite the unpleasantness with that horrible lawyer—

BRUFF
Miss Clack, before you continue, it is imperative, at this juncture, that I mention what happened to me the next morning.

CLACK
Do as you must, Mr. Bruff. *(She exits)*

BRUFF
(To the audience) I'll be brief, I assure you. Arriving at my office the following day, I found an unexpected visitor.

(BRUFF crosses to his office, where INDIAN #1 awaits him)

INDIAN #1
Good day, sir. I was recommended to you by Mr. Septimus Luker. *(Producing a small ebony casket inlaid with jewels)* I have come to ask you to lend me money. And I leave this as assurance that my debt will be repaid.

BRUFF
I believe there's been some mistake. I don't know Mr. Luker. Why did he not advance the money?

INDIAN #1
He informed me, sir, that he had no money to lend, and sent me to you.

BRUFF
I'm sorry, but Mr. Luker is quite mistaken in referring you here. I never make loans to strangers.

INDIAN #1
(Bowing, he takes up his box and crosses to exit. At the door, he stops) Supposing, sir, you had lent me the money... in what space of time would it have been customary for me to pay it back?

BRUFF
According to the usual course pursued in this country: one year.

(INDIAN #1 bows and exits)

BRUFF
(To the audience) My heart had barely stopped racing before Mr. Luker himself appeared in the flesh...

(LUKER enters, vulgar and cringing)

ACT TWO

LUKER
Please forgive me, sir. That man called upon me this morning and was clearly one of those stinking Indians who assaulted me. I was paralyzed with fear, and believed my last hour had come.

BRUFF
Did he threaten you?

LUKER
Well, not as such. He asked for money and produced a small casket. I thought it was a trick, so I said I had no money to lend. He demanded to know the best person to apply to for a loan. In the extremity of my terror, yours was the first name which occurred to me. Please forgive me!

BRUFF
Well, no harm done, I reckon. But, wait; did he say anything in particular, before quitting your office?

LUKER
Yes! It was quite unaccountable. He wanted to know the typical length of a loan in our country. *(He exits)*

BRUFF
(To the audience) What did this mean, I wondered?

(CLACK enters)

CLACK
And I'm sure we'll hear all about your clever theories soon enough. But, if I may continue?

BRUFF
Of course, Miss Clack. *(He exits)*

CLACK
(To the audience) Ah, the spiritual atmosphere feels

clear once more. Dear friends, we may go on. The morning after the signing of Lady Julia's Will, when I reflected on the religious riches I had scattered in the house of my wealthy aunt, I felt as free from all anxiety as if I had been a child again. Until Lady Verinder's servant girl arrived.

(PENELOPE arrives with a package for CLACK containing all the tracts she had left behind)

PENELOPE
My lady begs to return your tracts. Her doctor forbids the reading of them.

CLACK
(With a gasp) I must see my aunt at once!

PENELOPE
She's gone for a drive with Miss Rachel and Mr. Ablewhite.

CLACK
Mr. Ablewhite is with them? But, we have the Mothers'–Small–Clothes–Conversion Society! And then a meeting for the British–Ladies'–Servants'–Sunday–Sweetheart–Supervision Society!

PENELOPE
Sorry, Miss, I don't know what to say. *(PENELOPE exits)*

CLACK
(To the audience) Our Christian Hero was revealing one of the most awful backslidings of modern times. And what was to be done for my aunt? Salvation by tracts had failed. What to try next? Salvation by Little Notes! I spent all afternoon preparing letters to Lady Verinder. As letters they

would excite no suspicion; they would be opened; and, once opened, might be read. Armed with over a dozen, I arrived at my aunt's. I was told she was resting, but I went in regardless. *(She stealthily enters the library and hides letters about the room. Then, footsteps are heard in the hallway)* Who could be approaching at this hour?

(CLACK slips into a hiding place as GODFREY enters)

GODFREY
(Muttering to himself) I'll do it today!

CLACK
(To the audience) What would he do? Something even more deplorably unworthy of him? Would he apostatize from the faith? Had we seen the last of his angelic smile in the committee-room?

(CLACK is about to step out and confront GODFREY when RACHEL enters)

RACHEL
What are you doing here, Godfrey? I thought you were off to some ball tonight.

GODFREY
I'm so much happier here, with you.

RACHEL
It's hard to get over one's bad habits, but do try to get over the habit of flattering me.

GODFREY
I have never flattered you, Rachel. Love, dearest, always speaks the truth.

RACHEL
Remember what I said in the country; we are to be cousins, nothing more.

GODFREY
I forget every time I see you.

RACHEL
Then don't see me.

GODFREY
I forget every time I think of you. I have lost every interest in life, but my interest in you. A transformation has come over me which I cannot account for. My charity work is now an unendurable nuisance to me; and when I see a Ladies' Committee, I wish myself at the opposite end of the earth!

RACHEL
Would it cure you to know that I am the wretchedest girl living? It's true. What greater wretchedness can there be than to live degraded in your own mind?

GODFREY
Rachel! I know the disappearance of your birthday gift may seem strange, but—

RACHEL
If the true story of the Moonstone ever comes to light, it will be known that I accepted a dreadful responsibility, but it will be clear that I did nothing wrong! You have misunderstood me, Godfrey. I must speak plainer. Suppose you were in love with some other woman. And suppose you discovered that woman to be utterly unworthy of you?

GODFREY
Yes?

RACHEL
And, suppose, in spite of that, you couldn't tear

her from your heart? No! Don't ask his name! He doesn't know what I have told you, and never will. Oh, Godfrey, I have sunk to my rightful place in your estimation, now, haven't I?

(RACHEL breaks down into tears. GODFREY falls to his knees at her feet)

GODFREY
Noble creature! I implore you: let the cure of your wounded heart be my care. Rachel, will you honor me – will you bless me – by being my wife?

RACHEL
You must be mad!

GODFREY
I don't ask for your love; not yet. For now, I will be content with your affection and regard. Let the rest be left to Time, which heals wounds even as deep as yours.

RACHEL
Don't tempt me, Godfrey; I am wretched and reckless enough as it is.

GODFREY
Forget your troubles and marry the man now at your feet, who prizes you above all other women on the face of the earth.

RACHEL
You won't hurry me, Godfrey? You won't ask for more than I can give?

GODFREY
My angel! I only ask you to give me yourself.

RACHEL
Then take me.

(They embrace closely)

CLACK
(To the audience) I tried to close my eyes before it happened, but I was too late.

(RACHEL and GODFREY kiss)

CLACK
(To the audience) Words cannot express the horror I felt.

(PENELOPE enters in tears)

PENELOPE
Miss Rachel! Where have you been?

RACHEL
I've been right here. What's happened?

PENELOPE
It's your mother, Miss! Come quickly! *(She exits, followed by RACHEL and GODFREY)*

CLACK
(To the audience) I shall spare you the even more horrible scene which followed. But allow me to inform you that my aunt was no more. *(She presents several tracts)* If you wish, I have copious extracts on hand which may shed some spiritual light on trying events such as these.

(FRANKLIN enters)

FRANKLIN
With respect, Miss Clack, reading from this species of literature is not necessary. Please limit yourself to your own experience of events.

CLACK

Mr. Blake, I am a Christian, and it is, therefore, quite impossible for you to offend me, however hard you may try. I have learnt Perseverance in the School of Adversity.

FRANKLIN
Please continue with your narrative, and I shall... persecute you no further. *(He exits)*

CLACK
(To the audience) Lady Julia's death left Rachel in the care of her uncle Ablewhite. Mr. Godfrey informed his father of his feelings, and within days their engagement was public. Several weeks later, Rachel summoned little Me to help pass the idle hours.

(RACHEL enters the Ablewhite sitting room, wearing mourning black. CLACK joins her)

RACHEL
Drusilla, I was in the habit of speaking very rudely to you in the past. I hope you will forgive me. My mother's friends were not always my friends. But now that I have lost her, my heart turns for comfort to the people she liked. *(She exits)*

CLACK
(To the audience) In hope of doing Good Work upon this poor woman, I visited daily, bringing my most precious publication: The Life, Letters, and Labours of Miss Jane Ann Stamper, forty–fourth edition; which bore marvelous appropriateness to Rachel's situation. I kept it by me and waited for the perfect opportunity to read it to her. A week later we were visited by Mr. Bruff, who took Rachel for a walk in the Park.

(RACHEL enters, arm in arm with BRUFF)

BRUFF
(To RACHEL) Are you sure of your resolution?

RACHEL
Quite sure.

(BRUFF exits)

CLACK
Did he have bad news for you?

RACHEL
On the contrary, it was news I needed to hear.

CLACK
I suppose that must mean word of Mr. Godfrey?

RACHEL
I shall never marry Mr. Godfrey Ablewhite!

CLACK
What can you possibly mean?

(BRUFF enters)

BRUFF
(To the audience) My fair friends, before Miss Clack completes her... contribution to this story, I simply must throw some light on the situation here, for Rachel had a reason for breaking off her engagement, and I was at the bottom of it. If I may, Miss Clack.

CLACK
By all means, proceed, Mr. Bruff. I'm quite accustomed to these indignities being heaped upon me. *(She exits)*

BRUFF

(To the audience) On Lady Verinder's death, her Will was placed into the Commons in the usual way. Now, I have friends in that office, and shortly thereafter, warning reached me of unusual goings-on. Concern for Rachel decided my course of action.

(BRUFF joins RACHEL and they walk in the Park)

BRUFF
Will you forgive an old friend of the family, if I ask whether your heart is set on this marriage?

RACHEL
I am marrying in despair, Mr. Bruff, on the chance of dropping into some sort of stagnant happiness which may reconcile me to the rest of my life.

BRUFF
His heart must be set on the marriage at any rate?

RACHEL
He says so, and I suppose I ought to believe him.

BRUFF
It sounds strange to my old-fashioned ears to hear you speak of your future husband as if you doubted his sincerity.

RACHEL
Mr. Bruff, you have something to tell me about Godfrey. Say it.

BRUFF
Your mother's Will has been examined at the Commons.

RACHEL
There's nothing to be contested, is there? Who

asked for it?

BRUFF
Skipp and Smalley, under instructions from their client... Godfrey Ablewhite.

RACHEL
He's investigating the estate? What does this mean?

BRUFF
Well, he's plainly revealed his mercenary intent in this engagement. Fortunately, your mother's excellent sense, and my long experience, combined to guard you from just such an opportunist. The houses in London and Yorkshire will fall to you when you marry, but neither you nor your husband can raise sixpence on the property.

RACHEL
Will Godfrey keep the engagement now that he knows?

BRUFF
I can't say. This may only be a misunderstanding. But if he stands in need of raising a large sum quickly... I'm sorry to burden you with this so soon after your mother's passing.

RACHEL
No, I am deeply grateful for your kindness.

RACHEL
I shall let it be known that I have thought it over, and I believe it best for both of us if we part. *(She exits)*

BRUFF & CLACK
(To the audience) Later that day—
BRUFF
(To CLACK) My apologies. The floor is yours, Miss

Clack. *(He exits)*

CLACK
(To the audience) Keeping strictly within the limits of my own personal experience, I have next to relate that Rachel and I were soon surprised by the sudden arrival of Godfrey Ablewhite's father.

(CLACK joins RACHEL as MR. ABLEWHITE storms in, followed by BRUFF and PENELOPE)

ABLEWHITE
Rachel! Some weeks ago, my son informed me that you engaged yourself to him. Is it possible that he misinterpreted your intentions?

RACHEL
No; I did consent to marry him.

ABLEWHITE
Ah, I see. You've had a lovers' quarrel and my idiot son took it the wrong way. I should have known.

RACHEL
We have had no quarrel.

ABLEWHITE
Come now, don't be hard on Godfrey! Has he said something stupid, again? He was always clumsy from a child, but he means well.

RACHEL
Uncle, I proposed breaking off our marriage engagement, and he agreed. It's as simple as that.

ABLEWHITE
(Growing furious) What complaint do you have against Godfrey?

BRUFF

(To RACHEL) You are not bound to answer that question.

ABLEWHITE
(In a rage, to BRUFF) Your interference, sir, has not been asked for! *(To RACHEL)* What has my son done? I have a right to know!

RACHEL
You have the only explanation which I think it necessary to give.

ABLEWHITE
So, then, in plain English, it's your sovereign pleasure to jilt my son?

BRUFF
Now, sir—

ABLEWHITE
If Godfrey doesn't feel this insult, I do! My son isn't good enough for you? I knew it all along. It's the damned Verinder blood in you! *(In a rage, ABLEWHITE hurls a nearby piece of furniture)*

CLACK
Dear Mr. Ablewhite! *(Everyone freezes)* Permit me to draw your attention to some words. *(She presents her book)* Words of comfort, words of wisdom: the blessed, blessed words of Miss Jane Ann Stamper! Letter one thousand and one: "Peace in Families."

ABLEWHITE
Miss Jane Ann Stamper be damned! *(He takes the book from CLACK and throws it across the room)* Who invited this Rampant Spinster!? *(To CLACK)* Remove yourself at once!

RACHEL

But Miss Clack is here as my guest—

ABLEWHITE
And as for you, missy... don't think I haven't heard all the rumors. Not too proud to pawn that Moonstone of yours, are you? But you're still too damned high and mighty to marry my son. Get out! And may I never see you again as long as I live!

RACHEL
(Breaking down in tears) But you're the only family I have left!

ABLEWHITE
Not anymore, I'm not. I'm done with you! *(He exits)*

CLACK
(To RACHEL) How could your mother leave you in the care of that brute?

BRUFF
Because she believed in him; it was always her way to see the best in people. I never trusted him myself, and insisted that her Will empower me to appoint you a new guardian, if necessary. My dear, will you honor my wife and me by staying under our roof, until we wise people can settle what's to be done next?

CLACK
Appoint me guardian!

RACHEL
You are very kind, Drusilla. But I think it will be best if I remain under Mr. Bruff's care.

CLACK
Oh, don't say so! *(Throwing her arms around RACHEL)* Rachel! Haven't you seen that my heart yearns to

make a Christian of you? Don't follow in Aunt Julia's footsteps! Think of the horror of dying unprepared!

RACHEL
For God's sake, think of my poor mother's useful, beautiful life! And you try to make me doubt that this woman, who was an angel on earth, is an angel now in heaven! Come away, Mr. Bruff! It stifles me to breathe the same air with this woman! *(She exits)*

BRUFF
You would have done better to keep your mouth shut, Clack. *(He bows and exits)*

PENELOPE
I'm only a poor servant, but I declare I'm ashamed of you! *(She exits)*

CLACK
(To the audience) There you see my lot in life: reviled by all, deserted by all. If only the Moonstone had never entered our lives! Its loss killed my aunt, destroyed my cousin's hope for salvation, and tore me from what little family I had left. I remained for some time, gathering my strength, until...

(GODFREY enters)

GODFREY
My dear Miss Clack, what a relief to see you! I'm sure you've heard about me and Rachel.

CLACK
What will you do now?

GODFREY
I shall return to my charity work, and my Ladies. What do I want with an income? I'm not wealthy

like the Verinders, but I can pay for my little lodging and my two coats a year. And what do I want with Rachel? She told me that she loves another man. A month ago I was pressing her rapturously to my bosom. Now, the happiness of knowing that I shall never do so again intoxicates me like strong liquor. Can you account for it, dear friend?

CLACK
If I may speak as a spiritual physician, this is the welcome reappearance of your finer nature, after being humbled by an all-wise Providence.

GODFREY
Yes! I am as a lost man emerging from darkness into the light.

CLACK
You will receive a most loving reception at the Mothers'-Small-Clothes.

GODFREY
Ah! My grateful heart overflows, dear, dear friend.

(GODFREY *takes* CLACK's *hands and kisses them. She submits and, in an ecstasy of spiritual self-forgetfulness, embraces him, and nearly swoons*)

GODFREY
My dear Miss Clack, I must depart. But I shall see you soon. I promise. *(He exits)*

CLACK
(To the audience) Yet from that day forth, I never saw Godfrey Ablewhite again. Or Rachel, for that matter. But know that she has my forgiveness for insulting me. And when I die, to complete the return on my part of good for evil, she will have

The Life, Letters, and Labours of Miss Jane Ann Stamper, forty-fourth edition, left her as a legacy by my will.

(BRUFF enters as CLACK exits)

BRUFF
(To the audience) Well, my friends, Rachel came into my care, but I tell you, my heart was sore charged over the sufferings of her family. What would it take to bring these troubles to an end? My mind kept returning to the mystery of the Indian's visit to my office...

(INDIAN #1 appears)

INDIAN #1
Supposing, sir, you had lent me the money... in what space of time would it have been customary for me to pay it back? *(He exits)*

BRUFF
(To the audience) I examined this question from all sides, yet my unaided ingenuity proved unequal to grapple with it. Thankfully, I soon encountered the famous world traveler Mr. Murthwaite.

(MURTHWAITE enters)

MURTHWAITE
Let me ask a question: how does the conspiracy to seize the Moonstone now stand?

BRUFF
I can't say. The Indian plot is a mystery to me.

MURTHWAITE
It can only be a mystery to you because you have never seriously examined it. Tell me: which event

gave the Indians their first chance of seizing the diamond?

BRUFF
Colonel Herncastle's death.

MURTHWAITE
Naturally. So, they find a local accomplice to examine the Colonel's Will; they follow Mr. Blake through London and on to Yorkshire—

BRUFF
But why did they never make a move in the month before Rachel's birthday?

MURTHWAITE
Because they knew that the Moonstone would soon pass to Miss Verinder. So what was the safest course? To wait till it was in the hands of a helpless young girl. But its disappearance utterly paralyzed their plot. So far, so good. Now, when did the second chance of seizing the diamond offer itself?

BRUFF
The attacks on Mr. Luker and Godfrey Ablewhite. But how did they know about Luker?

MURTHWAITE
Because they were watching him carefully. In his report to the magistrate, you may recall that Luker mentioned a foreign workman in his employment, whom he had just dismissed...

BRUFF
Ah! Their accomplice, again!

MURTHWAITE
(He draws out his pocket–book) Before the Indians were released from confinement in Frizinghall, the

police came to me with a letter which had been sent to them. It was in Hindustani, and I translated it. I made a copy in my pocket-book.

BRUFF
(Reading from the book) By the Regent of the Night, whose seat is the Antelope, whose arms embrace the four corners of the earth: Brothers, turn your faces to the south, and come to me in the city by the muddy river. Mine own eyes have seen It.

MURTHWAITE
The god of the moon is represented as a four-armed deity, seated on an antelope.

BRUFF
And when the Indians were set free they came at once to London.

MURTHWAITE
But by the prompt transport of the stone to his banker's vault, Luker outwitted the conspirators, and the jewel was once more out of reach. So, what is their third chance of seizing it?

BRUFF
I see at last! The Indians believe, as we do, that the Moonstone has been pledged; and now – thanks to me! – they know the earliest time it can be redeemed from the bank!

MURTHWAITE
If the unknown person who pledged the Moonstone with Mr. Luker can redeem it in a year, the jewel will reemerge at the end of June, eighteen 'forty-nine. I shall be thousands of miles away at that date. But it may be worth your while to make a note of it. And to tread carefully.

BRUFF
You think something serious will happen?

MURTHWAITE
The Indians have been defeated twice running, but they won't be defeated a third time. I think I shall be safer among the fiercest jungles of Central Asia than I should be crossing the door of the bank with the Moonstone in my pocket. *(He exits)*

BRUFF
(To the audience) I did as he suggested and noted the date in my calendar.

(FRANKLIN enters as BRUFF exits)

FRANKLIN
(To the audience) Thank you, Mr. Bruff. Now then: one year later, in the spring of eighteen forty–nine, I was wandering the depths of Africa when word reached me that my father had died, and I was heir to his entire fortune. I returned at once to London. Having been wounded to the heart by Rachel's treatment, I went abroad resolved to forget her. But with the act of turning homeward, her influence recovered its hold on me and she was the first person I inquired after. But she refused to see me. Somehow, my unknown offence remained unpardoned in Rachel's mind. I wouldn't – I couldn't! – accept that position, and I became obsessed with discovering the cause of her silent enmity. I went to Yorkshire, resolved to take up the inquiry of the diamond again, and follow it to the bitter end. If time, pains, and money could do it, I would lay my hand on the thief who took the Moonstone!

(BETTEREDGE appears, dozing in a chair, Robinson

Crusoe on his chest. FRANKLIN crosses to him)

FRANKLIN
Betteredge! Has Robinson Crusoe informed you to expect me?

BETTEREDGE
As I live by bread, sir, here's what I was just reading: 'I stood like one Thunderstruck, or as if I had seen an Apparition.' If that isn't as much as to say: 'Expect the sudden appearance of Mr. Franklin,' there's no meaning in the English language! It's good to see you again, though I'm heartily sorry for the loss of your father. There have been sad changes here, too, since you left. The house is shut up, the servants are gone... Never mind! I'll cook you dinner; and make your bed— *(There is a knock at the door)* Come in.

(JENNINGS enters)

JENNINGS
I beg your pardon, Mr. Betteredge. I had no idea you were engaged. *(He hands a paper to BETTEREDGE, stopping to stare pointedly at FRANKLIN)* The list for next week.

FRANKLIN
What is that?

BETTEREDGE
The sick people who stand in need of a little wine. My lady always had a regular distribution of port among the infirm poor; and Miss Rachel wishes the custom to be kept up.

FRANKLIN
(To JENNINGS) I'm sorry; you look so familiar...

have we met before?

JENNINGS
Ezra Jennings, sir. Dr. Candy's assistant.

FRANKLIN
Ah, yes! How is the doctor?

BETTEREDGE
He never recovered from the illness he caught last year, leaving the birthday dinner. Lost his memory in the fever, they say.

JENNINGS
Indeed. We were both exposed to the elements on the ride home. But where I quickly recovered from the chill, he sank, hour by hour. For days, I remained at his side and treated him to the best of my ability. Towards sunset, the delirium came on. It lasted through the night, till the early morning hours when Death and I did battle over which should have the doctor. Finally there came a day when I knew I had saved him; and I own I broke down. But his memory never returned.

BETTEREDGE
Well, that will be all, Jennings. On your way.

(JENNINGS exits)

BETTEREDGE
Such a shame. All of Dr. Candy's work falls on him, now. Not much of it these days, except among the poor, and they can't help themselves; they must put up with that man.

FRANKLIN
You don't like him?

BETTEREDGE

Nobody likes him. Candy took him in with a very doubtful character. But enough of Ezra Jennings; I'm burning to know what's brought you down here.

FRANKLIN
It's the Moonstone. I have come to take up the inquiry again.

BETTEREDGE
Let the diamond be, Mr. Franklin! The cursed thing has misguided everybody who comes near it. How can you hope to succeed, when Sergeant Cuff himself made a mess of it?

FRANKLIN
My mind is made up, old friend. By–the–bye, I may want to speak with the Sergeant.

BETTEREDGE
He won't help you, sir. The great Cuff retired. He got a little cottage at Dorking and is up to his eyes in the growing of roses. But I believe I can help you pick up the trail of evidence. You remember poor Rosanna Spearman? She left a sealed letter behind her... addressed to you.

FRANKLIN
Why wasn't it forwarded to me?

BETTEREDGE
We didn't know where you went, sir.

FRANKLIN
Well, where is it, Betteredge? *(Noticing a growing restlessness in him)* Are you all right?

BETTEREDGE
I feel a disease coming on, sir. I don't want to alarm you, but you're certain to catch it before the day is

out.

FRANKLIN
The devil I am!

BETTEREDGE
Do you feel an uncomfortable heat at the pit of your stomach? And a nasty thumping at the top of your head? Not yet? Ah! It will lay hold of you soon, Mr. Franklin. I call it detective–fever; and I first caught it in the company of Sergeant Cuff.

(BETTERDGE gives FRANKLIN the letter. As he opens it and reads, ROSANNA appears)

ROSANNA
Sir, if you wish to know the meaning of my behavior to you, do as you are told here.

(As ROSANNA relates her instructions, FRANKLIN and BETTERDGE cross to the Shivering Sand)

ROSANNA
Go to the Shivering Sand at the turn of the tide. Walk out on the South Spit, till the beacon and the flagstaff above Cobb's Hole make a line together. Lay down on the rocks and feel down the edge overlooking the quicksand. Find the chain. And then pull.

(ROSANNA disappears as FRANKLIN pulls up the tin box by the length of chain. He opens the box to discover a letter sitting atop a rolled–up nightgown)

FRANKLIN
There's another letter, also in Rosanna's hand. *(Examining the nightgown)* And what's this…?

(CUFF appears)

CUFF

Find the article of dress with a smear of paint on it. Find out who it belongs to. Find that out, and you haven't far to look for the hand that has got the diamond. *(He exits)*

BETTEREDGE

For mercy's sake, sir, what is it? Detective–fever is killing me.

FRANKLIN

It's a nightgown, Betteredge. And, look, here's the smear of paint we sought for.

BETTEREDGE

Is it marked with the owner's name? What does it say?

FRANKLIN

(Reading the name inside the nightgown) Franklin Blake.

BLACKOUT

END OF ACT TWO

ACT III

(FRANKLIN appears, in the Verinder sitting room. BETTEREDGE pours two glasses of grog. The nightgown and letter sit on a nearby table)

FRANKLIN
(To the audience) So, there I was: in a situation without parallel: on the undeniable evidence of a paint stain, I had discovered myself as the thief. And what did I do? Deny the impossibility? Turn myself in? No. I accepted shelter in a house which I had resolved never to enter again, and tippled spirits with an old servant. This part of the story brings me terrible pain, but it leads us forward on the journey from darkness to the light.

BETTEREDGE
Now, Mr. Franklin, there's one thing certain, at any rate... *(Pointing an accusatory finger at the nightgown)* That thing's a liar.

FRANKLIN
The paint and the name on the nightgown are facts.

BETTEREDGE
Facts? Bah! Foul play!

FRANKLIN
Was I drunk on the night of Rachel's birthday?

BETTEREDGE
You! Why, it's the greatest defect of your character that you drink as little as you do!

FRANKLIN
But it was a special occasion—

BETTEREDGE
Well, at the end of the evening we persuaded you to have a drop of brandy and water.

FRANKLIN
I'm not used to brandy. Perhaps—

BETTEREDGE
Wait, sir. I knew you were not used to it, so I poured you only half a glass and drowned it in nigh on a tumbler-full of water. A child couldn't have got drunk on it.

FRANKLIN
As a boy, did I ever walk in my sleep?

BETTEREDGE
You, sir? You never did such a thing in your life!

FRANKLIN
Damn. Those are the only explanations I can see for me getting the paint on my nightgown without knowing it.

BETTEREDGE
If we are to believe the nightgown – which I don't – you not only smeared the paint without knowing it, but you also took the diamond without knowing it. Is that right, so far?

FRANKLIN
Go on.

BETTEREDGE
So, say you were drunk, or walking in your sleep. That accounts for the theft. But the diamond was taken to London and pledged to Mr. Luker. Did you do that without knowing it, too? It doesn't make sense. But what about the letter? In justice to Rosanna, let's see what it says.

(ROSANNA enters as FRANKLIN reads the letter)

FRANKLIN
(Reading from the letter) Sir, a confession of great misery may sometimes be made in very few words.

ROSANNA
(Continuing) Mine can be made in three: I love you. Do you remember when you surprised us at the sands that day? You were like a prince in a fairy tale, a lover in a dream. Something that felt like the happy life I had never known leapt up in me the instant I set eyes on you. If you knew how I would cry all night with the misery of your indifference towards me, you would pity me perhaps. You would pity me less, if you knew how I hated Miss Rachel. My work was to tidy your room. It was the happiest hour in my day. I used to kiss the pillow on which your head had rested. And you have never had your clothes folded as nicely as I folded them for you.

FRANKLIN
I never noticed...

ROSANNA
The morning after the robbery, I found your nightgown on the bed; and there was the stain of paint on it. I didn't want this evidence to be found and point back to you, so I took the nightgown and made another exactly like it before Saturday laundry. But the excitement of my discovery turned my head. I was consumed by a need to see you, to make you speak to me. But, oh, sir, how my courage cooled as you continued to distrust me, when I was risking everything to keep your secret safe.

FRANKLIN
(*Handing BETTEREDGE the letter*) Read the rest yourself. I can't bear this, God help me.

BETTEREDGE
(*Reading from the letter*) Why couldn't I just talk to you? The truth is plain enough...

ROSANNA
(*Continuing*) I loved you with all my heart and soul but I'm such a plain girl; only a housemaid; what could you ever see in me? I should have destroyed the nightgown. But I couldn't destroy the only thing which proved I had saved you from discovery! So, I hid it at the place I knew best: the Shivering Sand. And what now? Now, I shall make one last attempt to speak to you. If I fail, there will be the end of my efforts... and my life. Don't blame yourself, if it ends this way. But when you find out what I have done for you, will you say something kind of me then, in the same gentle way you speak to Miss Rachel? If you do, and if there are such things

as ghosts, I believe I will hear it, and be at peace.

FRANKLIN
So many times, she attempted to speak to me...

BETTEREDGE
Sir, leave her miserable story behind you now. There are no such things as ghosts, and no part of her remains to feel your sorrows over her tale.

FRANKLIN
I wonder whether you're right, Betteredge.

(BETTEREDGE and ROSANNA exit. FRANKLIN crosses to join BRUFF in his sitting room)

BRUFF
It's a question of evidence. The name proves the nightgown to be yours. And the paint proves the nightgown to have made the smear on Rachel's door. But there's no proof that you wore it when the diamond was stolen. If Rachel suspects you on the evidence of the nightgown only, odds are it was Rosanna who showed it to her. Her own letter confesses that she was jealous of Rachel. She would have done anything to tear the two of you apart.

FRANKLIN
But what if I did wear the nightgown?

BRUFF
We must figure out a way to make Rachel speak.

FRANKLIN
I will talk to her.

BRUFF
You! But how will you see her?

FRANKLIN
She was, for some time, a guest at your house. May I venture to suggest – if nothing was said about me beforehand – that I might surprise her here?

BRUFF
I tell you fairly, I don't trust your discretion, or your temper. But I do trust that Rachel preserves, in some corner of her heart, a certain perverse weakness for you. I hope she will live to thank me for turning traitor. Consider me your accomplice. *(He exits)*

FRANKLIN
(To the audience) And so the trap was laid. The next day, Mr. Bruff invited Rachel to visit his family, but left the place empty for me.

(RACHEL enters)

RACHEL
Mr. Bruff? Hello? Is anyone here? *(RACHEL sees FRANKLIN. For a moment, they confront each other in stunned silence)*

FRANKLIN
Rachel.

RACHEL
You miserable, heartless coward! After all you have done, you find your way to me like this?

FRANKLIN
What have I done?

RACHEL
I have kept your infamy a secret. And I have suffered the consequences.

FRANKLIN
Did Rosanna Spearman show you the nightgown? Yes, or no?

RACHEL
Are you mad?

FRANKLIN
You have done me an infamous wrong! You suspect me of stealing your diamond. I have a right to know why!

RACHEL
Suspect you?! You villain, I saw you take the diamond with my own eyes!

(FRANKLIN staggers back in shock)

RACHEL
Why did you come here?

FRANKLIN
(He takes RACHEL's hand) Rachel, I can't explain the contradiction in what I am going to tell you. I can only speak the truth, and ask you to trust me. You say you saw me take the diamond. Before God, I declare that I only now believe I took it for the first time!

RACHEL
Let go of me.

FRANKLIN
Tell me what happened.

RACHEL
Why go back to it?

FRANKLIN
You and I are the victims of some monstrous delu-

sion wearing the mask of truth. If we look at that night together, we may end in understanding each other yet. Begin after we wished each other good night. Did you go directly to bed?

RACHEL
I did; but I couldn't sleep. I was thinking of you. At one o'clock, I lit a candle, and was going to my sitting room for a book. I had just opened the bedroom door when I saw a light approaching. I blew out my candle, and then I saw… I saw you.

FRANKLIN
Were my eyes open?

RACHEL
Yes. They were bright; brighter than usual. You looked about, as if you were afraid, and then you went directly to the cabinet. You put your candle atop it and opened drawers until you found the diamond.

FRANKLIN
Are you sure I took it out?

RACHEL
I saw the gleam of the stone between your fingers. Then you took up the candle again and left the room. Your light disappeared, your footsteps died away, and I was left alone in the dark. Well? You asked, and I have answered. You made me hope something from all this. What have you to say now?

FRANKLIN
If you had only done me the common justice to explain yourself—

RACHEL
I spared you, when my heart was breaking, when my own character was at stake; and you turn on me now?

(FRANKLIN crosses to exit)

RACHEL
You will not skulk out like a dog. You shall hear me, and see whether I tried to do you justice or not. Despite what I had seen, I refused to believe you were really a thief. I left the sitting room open all morning, hoping with all my heart that you would return the diamond. When you didn't, I gave you every opportunity of owning the truth. But what did you do? You fetched the police!

FRANKLIN
But if you had spoken out at the time—

RACHEL
You would have been disgraced for life! If I had spoken, you would have denied it, as you are denying it now! I shrank from the horror of seeing you lie, after the horror of watching you thieve. You talk as if this was a misunderstanding which a few words might have set right. Well, the misunderstanding is at an end. And is the thing set right? No! *(She embraces FRANKLIN)*

FRANKLIN
Let me go, Rachel. It will be better for both of us.

RACHEL
If you needed money, I would have given it to you. I would have pledged the diamond myself. But your father's dead and you are a rich man, now. You don't need me anymore. Are you afraid

I'll say what I know? I can't! I can't tear you out of my heart, even now! You may trust in my shameful weakness.

FRANKLIN
I will prove to you that I did not do this thing. Or you shall never see me again!

RACHEL
Franklin, I forgive you! Can you not forgive me?

(FRANKLIN exits, meeting BRUFF)

FRANKLIN
Ah, Mr. Bruff, how can I deny the hateful Fact any longer, when I've heard it from her own lips?

BRUFF
We must forget what happened in the past and look to what we can discover in the future.

FRANKLIN
But the whole thing is a matter of the past!

BRUFF
Answer me this: we know the Moonstone was pledged to Mr. Luker, and we know that you are not the person who pledged it. Do we know who did?

FRANKLIN
No.

BRUFF
Exactly. Now observe. At the end of the month, a year will have elapsed from the time when the jewel was pledged. The person who pawned it may appear to redeem it. If he does, Mr. Luker must himself take the diamond out of the vault. I propose setting a watch at the bank.

FRANKLIN
Well now, I admit that's a fine idea... but it means waiting.

BRUFF
Only about a fortnight. *(He exits)*

FRANKLIN
(To the audience) My existence was unendurable without doing something towards clearing my character at once. I sent a letter to Sergeant Cuff, but he was gone to Ireland; some gardener had discovered something new in the growing of roses. After that, I was at a loss. I stayed up all night, smoking, and building up theories – one more profoundly improbable than another – until I became lost in the mist of my own metaphysics. I kept returning to the birthday dinner, searching for people to help me piece together this puzzle. But it was odd: I seemed to remember that evening through a haze. I could barely recall who was there.

(During the following, the guests take their places at the birthday dinner and re-enact it in dumb show as FRANKLIN walks amongst them. After he discusses each guest, they leave the table)

FRANKLIN
(To the audience) Aunt Julia was gone now. Miss Clack? I might have to seek her out, God help me. Mr. Murthwaite? He couldn't help me. He was gone to the far East again. And Godfrey... No, he'd left town as well. After Rachel, he proposed to another young heiress. And, again, the engagement had broken off. But then he suddenly found himself the recipient of five thousand pounds, left by a rich old lady at the Mothers'–Small–

Clothes–Society. He took the legacy and went to the Continent, telling everyone he'd be away at least three months.

(FRANKLIN looks at RACHEL for a moment, then she departs)

FRANKLIN
(To the audience) There was no one left but Dr. Candy. I took the first train back to Yorkshire.

(CANDY appears in his sitting room and FRANKLIN joins him. CANDY is utterly changed: his eyes are dim, his figure shrunken. JENNINGS sees to CANDY's comfort)

FRANKLIN
I hope I'm not intruding.

JENNINGS
Actually, sir, the doctor is not well these days—

CANDY
Nonsense, Jennings! *(To FRANKLIN)* I am heartily glad to see you... er...

JENNINGS
Mr. Blake.

CANDY
Ah! Yes! I have often thought of you, Mr. Blake. How may I serve you, sir?

FRANKLIN
Actually, Dr. Candy, do you remember the Indian diamond, from a year ago? I was hoping you could lend me the assistance of your memory...

(CANDY's eyes go watery and vague at the mention of the Moonstone, but then he brightens suddenly)

CANDY
I wanted to say something to you...

FRANKLIN
Yes?

CANDY
I had something to say to you... very important... *(He falls silent)*

FRANKLIN
Was it about the night of Rachel's birthday dinner?

CANDY
That's it! The birthday dinner! *(He rises triumphantly to his feet, then collapses in frustration over his faded memory)* It was very pleasant, wasn't it? I am so glad we have met again. Good day... *(He wanders out of the room)*

FRANKLIN
No, Dr. Candy, wait: you're the only one who can help me!

JENNINGS
Please, sir; let him go. His knowledge of events before his illness is gone, poor man.

FRANKLIN
Is his memory never any better?

JENNINGS
Sadly, no. Yet, perhaps we should all be happier, if we could forget!

FRANKLIN
Is there nothing we can do to assist him? He knows something... locked away somewhere in his mind. You saw it as well as I did.

JENNINGS
May I ask what your interest is in all this?

FRANKLIN
Why? Did he say something to you? What do you know?

JENNINGS
Well... it may be possible to trace his lost recollection, without appealing to the doctor himself.

FRANKLIN
How?

JENNINGS
During his illness, I wrote down his delirious wanderings. And then I treated them like a child's puzzle: all confusion to begin with; but they may be brought into order, if you can find the way. I pieced his ramblings together until I found their meaning, and discovered that Dr. Candy's mind was intensely obsessed with something to do with you.

FRANKLIN
What was it? Tell me!

JENNINGS
Not until you tell me why you need the information. Sir, remember how I obtained it! Dr. Candy was so helplessly dependent upon me!

FRANKLIN
I don't even know you. Why should I take you into my confidence?

JENNINGS
Because I shall admit you into mine. I'll tell you the truth about how I came to live in Dr. Candy's house. All I wanted was a simple life. But when

I found my heart's dear love, her family couldn't accept me. Gypsy, they called me; tinker, and worse. They lashed out with the vilest of slanders and struck down my reputation forever. I was forced from my profession, torn from the woman I loved. Evil report travels patiently, and far. It followed me from place to place, for decades. It ended in my drifting here, and meeting with Dr. Candy. I told him everything. He said, 'I believe in you, and I pity you. If you will risk slander following you here, I will risk it too.' God Almighty bless him!

FRANKLIN
Has the slander died out?

JENNINGS
No. But when it finds me here, I shall be dead. I suffer from an incurable internal condition. I should have let the agony of it kill me long ago, but I still wish to provide for a lady I shall never see again. The only effectual means I've found to resist the disease is... opium. To that merciful drug I am indebted for a respite from death. But the constant pain has forced me from the use of opium to the abuse of it. My nerves are shattered; my nights are a horror. The end is not far off now. Let it come.

FRANKLIN
Why are you telling me this?

JENNINGS
Because I want you to trust me, knowing that you speak to a dying man. And if the secret locked away in Dr. Candy's mind can do some good in this world, it is my duty to bring it into the light. But I must know I can trust you.

FRANKLIN
(To the audience) What else could I do? I told him the whole story from beginning to end.

JENNINGS
Were your nerves out of order, at this time last year?

FRANKLIN
Yes. I'd left off smoking and was sleeping very badly.

JENNINGS
Was the birthday night an exception?

FRANKLIN
It was.

JENNINGS
And was there a dispute with Dr. Candy, at the birthday dinner, over his profession?

FRANKLIN
Yes! I believe some foolish wrangle took place.

JENNINGS
And was the Moonstone the subject of conversation immediately before you retired?

FRANKLIN
Yes!

JENNINGS
(He collects a pile of written notes and hands them to FRANKLIN) Mr. Blake, these notes prove to me now that you took the diamond in a state of trance produced by opium, and that the opium was taken from Lady Verinder's medicine chest by Dr. Candy and given to you, without your knowledge, as a refutation of your words at the birthday dinner.

FRANKLIN
What the devil?

JENNINGS
Read the notes. Then I have something to propose to you.

FRANKLIN
(Reading the notes) Mr. Blake... down a peg... confesses... can't sleep at night... show him!... wants sleep?... Lady Verinder's medicine chest... laudanum... five-and-twenty minims... without his knowing it... Well, Mr. Blake?... what about medicine now? *(He returns the notes to JENNINGS)* By God, I believe you're right! But how did he give me the opium?

JENNINGS
I can't say. Nothing on that subject passed Dr. Candy's lips, all through his illness. But let's proceed to matters of more immediate importance. Are you willing to try a bold experiment?

FRANKLIN
Tell me what to do, and I'll do it!

JENNINGS
You shall do this, Mr. Blake: you shall steal the diamond, unconsciously, for the second time, in the presence of witnesses whose testimony is beyond dispute. Have you resumed smoking?

FRANKLIN
For nearly a year.

JENNINGS
Will you give it up again? Suddenly, mind! As you did before?

FRANKLIN
I will.

JENNINGS
If we can return your nerves to the same state in which the opium found you last year, a repetition of the dose may lead to a repetition of the result.

FRANKLIN
But, wait; I don't understand the effect of the laudanum on me: walking around, opening drawers. I thought opium sent you to sleep.

JENNINGS
A common error! I am, at this moment, exerting my intelligence, such as it is, under the influence of a dose ten times larger than that which Dr. Candy administered to you. Opium has two actions: a stimulating influence first, and a sedative influence afterwards. Under the stimulating influence, the latest impressions on your mind become intensified. Any apprehension you had about the Moonstone would have impelled you into action.

FRANKLIN
That explains why I took the diamond: I was trying to protect it, not steal it!

JENNINGS
Precisely! Then later, as the sedative action took hold, you would have fallen into a deep sleep, waking up absolutely ignorant of what you had done.

FRANKLIN
But what did I do with the jewel after Rachel saw me leave the room with it?

JENNINGS
That is the purpose of my experiment. You may repeat, under the second dose of opium, what you did with the stone, and its hiding place will be revealed!

FRANKLIN
Hiding place? But the Moonstone is in London, in Luker's bank.

JENNINGS
How did it get there?

FRANKLIN
Well... nobody knows, that's the problem.

JENNINGS
Have you any evidence to prove that the Moonstone was taken to London? Mr. Luker declares he never heard of it. The Indians assume he's lying, and you assume the Indians are right. I believe the stone is still hidden in the Verinder house, and all I say is, my view is possible. What more can be said for yours?

FRANKLIN
I confess you stagger me. Do you object to my telling Mr. Bruff what you have said?

JENNINGS
On the contrary, I insist. Tell Sergeant Cuff, as well. *(He shakes FRANKLIN's hand)* If I can repair the mischief caused by Dr. Candy and clear your name – if I can do you this service, Mr. Blake, I shall feel it like a faint gleam of sunshine, on a long and cloudy day.

FRANKLIN
(To the audience, drawing forth the journal he set aside

at the beginning of the play) Owing to my condition at the time, the next ten days are placed on record from the journal of Ezra Jennings. Not long after the events of our story, his incurable disease claimed his life. But his spirit lives on in this diary, which Dr. Candy was good enough to part with. Out of respect for all he did for me, I will let Jennings tell you, in his own words, how the opium experiment was tried.

(FRANKLIN reads from the journal; as he does, JENNINGS addresses the audience)

JENNINGS
(To the audience) Our preparations began with a flurry of letters, some sent by Mr. Blake...

(BRUFF and CUFF appear, separately)

BRUFF
I strongly disapprove of your course of action, young man.

CUFF
Mr. Blake, I beg permission to remain in retirement, surrounded by the peaceful horticultural attractions of a country life.

JENNINGS
(To the audience) Others, by necessity, sent by me...

(RACHEL appears)

RACHEL
Your letter has satisfied me of Mr. Blake's innocence, without the slightest need of putting your assertion to the proof. But if you wish, my mother's house is at your disposal. Betteredge shall obey your every command!

JENNINGS
(To the audience) Despite continual interruption from patients, and from pain, the letters continued...

CUFF
Yet, if you are aware of any serious mistake in last year's inquiry, I will consider it a duty to place myself at your disposal when I return from Ireland. *(He exits)*

JENNINGS
(To the audience) We told the Sergeant all that had happened.

BRUFF
After consulting several eminent physicians, I have determined to join you, albeit under protest. *(He exits)*

JENNINGS
(To the audience) Excellent! A skeptic is just what we need.

RACHEL
I do wish, however, to be present when the experiment is tried, if I may. *(She exits)*

JENNINGS
(To the audience) Miss Verinder must not be seen by Mr. Blake. But I cannot find it in my heart to disappoint her. I have proposed that she arrive at the house secretly. After I have seen Mr. Blake safely to bed, she can watch with the rest of us. Mr. Blake reports of...

FRANKLIN
(To the audience) Miserable, restless nights and a total failure of appetite. *(He exits)*

JENNINGS
(To the audience) Exactly what happened last year, when he gave up his cigars. These are hopeful signs. Yet the vengeance of opium pursues me through frightful dreams: whirling through empty space while the beloved face I shall never see again rises before me, phosphorescent in the hideous darkness. But I must press on. *(Crossing into the Verinder house)* At last, we have reached the day of the experiment! We moved into the Verinder estate, dining at exactly the hour of the birthday dinner last year.

(BETTEREDGE enters)

BETTEREDGE
I have lived a goodish long time; and how does it all end? With a conjuring trick performed on Mister Franklin by a gypsy with a bottle of laudanum. And I'm to be conjurer's boy! *(JENNINGS makes to speak, but BETTEREDGE prevents him)* Not a word, Mr. Jennings! If Miss Rachel says, 'Do it,' it shall be done... even though I believe you to be a person with a head full of maggots! *(He exits)*

(BRUFF and RACHEL enter and RACHEL rushes to JENNINGS)

RACHEL
Mr. Jennings! If you only knew how happy your letters have made me.

JENNINGS
Miss Verinder. And Mr. Bruff, I presume. Miss Verinder has probably told you that I wish her presence in the house to be kept a secret.

BRUFF
I know that I am to hold my tongue, sir. Being

habitually silent on the subject of human folly, I am prepared to keep my lips closed on this occasion.

RACHEL
Oh, Mr. Jennings! Is he in good spirits? How does he bear the sight of the house, after last year? May I watch you pour out the laudanum? You must wonder at the interest I take in this.

JENNINGS
No. I dare say I thoroughly understand.

RACHEL
You have given me a new life. I love him. I have loved him from the first, even when I was thinking the worst of him.

(BETTEREDGE enters with a medicine chest)

JENNINGS
Ah! Lady Verinder's medicine chest.

BETTEREDGE
Begging your pardon. Mr. Franklin is preparing for bed and wishes to know where you are. Being under orders to deceive him, I have said I don't know. That, you will observe, was a lie.

RACHEL
Oh, Gabriel, don't be unkind.

JENNINGS
Now, Mr. Bruff, I will prepare the laudanum, and I must request you to witness me administer the dose.

BRUFF
If that is to be my role in this farce, so be it.

RACHEL
May I pour out the water?

(JENNINGS measures out opium from the bottle and pours it into a glass. Then he hands it to RACHEL)

JENNINGS
Fill it till it is three parts full.

RACHEL
(She fills the glass, and the kisses it) When you give it to him, give it to him on that side!

JENNINGS
(Presenting a piece of crystal) You've got a hand in this, too. Place this where you put the Moonstone last year. It must all happen in the same way.

(RACHEL crosses to her sitting room and places the crystal in the Indian cabinet. JENNINGS joins FRANKLIN in his bedroom and gives him the glass, which he drinks before lying down in bed)

JENNINGS
(To FRANKLIN) Remember the Indians. Remember the Moonstone. Rachel's cabinet has no lock, and she sleeps alone, unprotected, in the adjacent room...

(JENNINGS draws the curtains around the bed so that BETTEREDGE and BRUFF are not in view by FRANKLIN as they enter to observe. Rain begins to fall. The scene is lit by a candle next to FRANKLIN's bed, and a candle burning in RACHEL's bedroom)

BETTEREDGE
(With excited anticipation, momentarily forgetting his dislike of JENNINGS) For the Lord's sake, sir, tell us when it will begin to work.

JENNINGS
Surely not before midnight. Now, be still. *(To the*

audience) It was five minutes to twelve when the symptoms of the laudanum first showed themselves.

(FRANKLIN sits up in bed. His eyes are open, but not present. He is in a state of agitation, nervous and perspiring. He mumbles low to himself, then trails off, seemingly about to fall back asleep)

FRANKLIN
(Nearly inaudible) Moonstone... what have I done...? Rachel... alone... no...

JENNINGS
(To the audience) I had just begun to fear that the experiment would fail, when...

FRANKLIN
(Suddenly rising to his feet) I should never have taken it out of the bank. It was safe there. *(Looking around in paranoia)* How do I know? The Indians may be hidden in the house. *(Walking towards the door)* Her cabinet doesn't even lock. *(Stopping abruptly)* Anybody might take it.

BRUFF
It's working!

(FRANKLIN takes up the candle and walks down the corridor into RACHEL's sitting room. JENNINGS, BRUFF, and BETTEREDGE follow at a distance. RACHEL puts out her candle and observes from her partially cracked bedroom door. FRANKLIN crosses to the cabinet, places his candle atop it, and opens drawers until he discovers the crystal. He takes it out and makes for the door, but gets no further than the sofa, where he sways and drops the crystal. He sinks onto the sofa and falls asleep)

JENNINGS
Blast!

RACHEL
(Rushing to FRANKLIN) Is he all right?

JENNINGS
(Checking on him) He's fine, though he'll probably sleep for the next six or seven hours.

RACHEL
I'll watch over him.

JENNINGS
The experiment has failed! It depended on his repeating exactly the proceedings of last year, but we have no more idea of where the Moonstone is than we did before.

BRUFF
Well, at least we've proved that Mr. Blake took the diamond unconsciously last year, under the influence of opium.

BETTEREDGE
But Miss Rachel told Mr. Franklin what she had seen. What if he simply acted it out as she described?

BRUFF
I met with several doctors in London, Mr. Betteredge, and they all concurred that his rational mind could never exert such control over the drug. I, for one, have been convinced.

JENNINGS
What now?

BRUFF
Now, it's back to London. I still believe that the

jewel is in Luker's bank. I have set a watch there and tomorrow, Mr. Blake and I will join the effort.

(BRUFF exits, followed by BETTEREDGE)

JENNINGS
(To the audience) Miss Verinder and I kept our watch together in silence. By eight o'clock Mr. Blake finally began to revive. And then I left them alone, together at last. *(He leaves the room, which falls dark behind him as FRANKLIN and RACHEL embrace)* Soon they will return to London, and the house will be empty again. Back to the dreadful battle between the opium and the pain. But God be praised for His mercy! I have seen a little sunshine. I have had a happy time. *(He exits)*

FRANKLIN
(To the audience, stepping forward with the journal) Rachel and I owe Ezra Jennings more than words can express. He was, as I think, a great man; though the world never knew him.

RACHEL
(Entering the scene with FRANKLIN) Must we return to the city?

FRANKLIN
If the diamond surfaces at the bank, we have to be there to recapture it.

RACHEL
But why? It wasn't uncle's to give in the first place, and I had no right to accept it. It nearly drove us apart. Can't we let it go?

FRANKLIN
Our lives have been upended, and they must be set

aright. That will only happen when we know the truth of the Moonstone. *(To the audience)* When we reached London, we were met by an unexpected visitor, newly arrived from Ireland.

(FRANKLIN and RACHEL cross to FRANKLIN's apartment, where they meet CUFF)

CUFF
Miss Verinder, please accept my apologies. All I can say is that I completely mistook the case. I made a mess of it.

FRANKLIN
Well, you have come in the nick of time to recover your reputation.

CUFF
Since I have retired, I have done with reputation, thank God! I am here, sir, in remembrance of Lady Verinder. Not a farthing is to pass to me. This is on honor. Now, I don't hold with Mr. Jennings that you hid the Moonstone. But I agree that you must certainly have taken it back to your room.

FRANKLIN
But what happened then?

CUFF
Have you no guess, sir? *(Taking a paper from the writing table, he writes on it, and seals it in an envelope)* I suspected the wrong person, last year; and I may be suspecting the wrong person now. *(He hands the sealed envelope to FRANKLIN)* Wait to open this, Mr. Blake, till we have the truth. And then compare the name of the guilty person with the name that I have written here.

(BRUFF enters)

BRUFF
Mr. Blake! And Sergeant Cuff!

FRANKLIN
Is there news?

BRUFF
Half an hour ago, my man at Luker's house spotted him leaving, and followed him directly to the bank. Luker is, right now, in the inner office.

FRANKLIN
He's going to withdraw the diamond! Let's go!

(They cross to the bank, where a great crowd has gathered)

CUFF
Any sign of the Indians?

BRUFF
None.

CUFF
They must have a spy somewhere...

RACHEL
(Spotting a SAILOR with a thick beard, wearing a dark coat and cap) What of that sailor?

BRUFF
(Observing a nervous WOMAN) Or that woman over there.

(LUKER enters)

FRANKLIN
There's Luker!

CUFF
Watch him. If he passes the diamond, he'll do it here.

(LUKER enters the crowd and bumps into the WOMAN and the SAILOR. After he makes contact with the WOMAN, she darts off. BRUFF grabs CUFF's arm)

BRUFF
Sergeant—

CUFF
Yes! I saw it, too!

(BRUFF, FRANKLIN, RACHEL, and CUFF proceed to the door, slowed by the crowd. On the street, the WOMAN exits one way and LUKER another, while the SAILOR slips off in a third direction)

CUFF
Mr. Bruff, follow the woman! I'll stick with Luker; you two with me.

FRANKLIN
But Sergeant, that sailor—

RACHEL
Did you see something?

FRANKLIN
Possibly...

BRUFF
Gentlemen, we're losing them!

CUFF
(To BRUFF) Go! *(To FRANKLIN)* Mr. Blake, remember: there's no such thing as a trifle. Don't ignore your instincts. Follow the sailor!

(BRUFF exits after the WOMAN and CUFF after LUKER, while FRANKLIN and RACHEL follow the SAILOR)

FRANKLIN
(To the audience) There was no denying it: Betteredge's "detective-fever" had consumed me utterly. We trailed the sailor to Shore Lane, where we spied a man dressed like a mechanic, also following our target.

(INDIAN #1, in disguise as a mechanic, joins the action, following the SAILOR in secret)

FRANKLIN
(To the audience) The hour was late, the neighborhood treacherous, and when the sailor stepped into a shabby public house, I sent Rachel home in a cab. Then I entered 'The Wheel of Fortune.'

(RACHEL kisses FRANKLIN and exits. The SAILOR approaches the LANDLADY in The Wheel of Fortune. INDIAN #1 slips in and listens to their conversation. FRANKLIN observes them all)

SAILOR
May I have a bed?

LANDLADY
Sorry love, we're all full.

SAILOR
No! I'll take anything. I'll sleep on the floor if I must!

LANDLADY
Well, I suppose I could open up Number Ten, if you want to wait. *(She exits)*

(The SAILOR sits at a table, while INDIAN #1 slips upstairs after the LANDLADY)

FRANKLIN
(To the audience) Unsure of who to watch at this stage, I stuck with the sailor. Several minutes later, angry voices were heard upstairs and the mechanic was hauled out by the landlady, exhibiting all the signs of being drunk.

(The LANDLADY drags INDIAN #1 in and tosses him out the front door)

LANDLADY
Out with you! I won't be having your kind here!

FRANKLIN
(To the audience) I was so struck by this sudden intoxication that I couldn't resist running out after the mechanic. He was reeling about in a most disgraceful manner, but the moment he turned the corner, he became completely sober.

(FRANKLIN follows INDIAN #1, who meets with INDIANS #2 and #3. INDIAN #1 removes his disguise and the three disappear into the night)

FRANKLIN
(To the audience) There, he met with two figures in Indian garb, and the three departed. It was obvious that I was at the center of something, but I couldn't watch the sailor and the Indians at the same time. I had to make a choice.

(FRANKLIN crosses to join BRUFF and CUFF)

BRUFF
So what did you do?

FRANKLIN
I watched the sailor until he went upstairs. Then, from the street, I waited until the light in his room went out. Only then did I dare return.

CUFF
Well done! You could do great things in my late profession, Mr. Blake.

FRANKLIN
What did you discover, on your parts?

BRUFF
Nothing. The woman was a dead end.

CUFF
I followed Luker back to his house. The shutters were put up and the doors bolted. And Luker never left. No, it's the sailor, all right. Luker definitely passed the diamond to him. And now the Indians are onto him. We must return to 'The Wheel of Fortune' at once!

(CUFF, FRANKLIN, and BRUFF cross to find the LANDLADY in a state of agitation)

LANDLADY
Who the devil are you?

CUFF
Madam, I'll advise you to keep your temper. I am Sergeant Cuff.

LANDLADY
Oh, sir, something terrible has happened.

CUFF
Relating to the sailor who slept here last night?

LANDLADY
Do you know him?

CUFF
I can't be certain till I see him.

LANDLADY
See him? That's the thing we haven't been able to do all morning. He left word, last night, to be called at six o' clock. He was called, but there was no getting an answer from him. We tried the door, but it's locked, and not a sound to be heard in the room!

CUFF
Could he leave the room in any way, without going out by the door?

LANDLADY
No, the room's an attic. But there is a trap door in the ceiling, leading out to the roof.

CUFF
Come, let's take a look!

(They cross to Room Number Ten. CUFF tries the door, to no avail. Combining their strength, BRUFF and FRANKLIN batter through it. Inside, the SAILOR lies motionless on the floor. Nearby, a wooden box sits empty atop a piece of paper. CUFF examines the SAILOR)

LANDLADY
Oh, God! He's dead!

CUFF
Quite so. Send for the nearest doctor, and fetch the police.

(The LANDLADY exits. BRUFF takes up the paper)

BRUFF

(Reading the paper) "Deposited by Mr. Septimus Luker, a valuable of great price, only to be given up on the personal application of Mr. Luker." But where's the stone?

CUFF

It's gone. And look at this... the sailor was disguised. *(He pulls at the SAILOR's hair and it comes off in his hand; it is a wig)* Mr. Blake, open the letter I gave you this morning.

(FRANKLIN produces the envelope and opens it as CUFF removes the SAILOR's beard, revealing...)

FRANKLIN

(Reading CUFF's note) "Mr. Godfrey Ablewhite."

CUFF

(To the audience) Since I led the subsequent inquiry into his life and death, I shall shine a light on the answers related to the late Mr. Ablewhite. We'll begin with the murder.

(During the following, the INDIANS are seen opening the trap door as GODFREY lies asleep in bed. INDIAN #1 is lowered into the room and takes the Moonstone from the box. As he is being raised back up through the ceiling, GODFREY wakes. GODFREY attacks the INDIAN, but in the struggle he is mortally wounded. The INDIANS exit, closing the trap door behind them, and leave GODFREY's body crumpled on the floor)

CUFF

(To the audience) When the trap door to the roof was examined, an aperture was found through which someone could have opened the door from

outside. Judging from the condition of the body, we have a reliable guess as to the circumstances of Mr. Ablewhite's death. As to the perpetrators, we know that the Indians wanted the diamond; a torn morsel of gold thread was found on the trap door, which experts declare to be of Indian manufacture; and on the next morning, three men, answering to their description, were seen leaving London by a steamer bound for Bombay. Passing next to Mr. Ablewhite himself...

(GODFREY rises)

CUFF

(To the audience) His life had two sides. The side on public display was that of a gentleman and philanthropist. The side kept in shadow was a man of pleasure, with a villa in the suburbs under a false name, and a lady in the villa, also taken under another name. How do we know this?

(LUKER appears and joins GODFREY)

CUFF

(To the audience) Before Mr. Luker took the stone from Ablewhite, he demanded to know the whole story. Luker revealed the details of their secret meeting only after Ablewhite's death, and only under considerable pressure from the law.

LUKER

(To GODFREY) But why on earth would you steal from your own family?

GODFREY

Several years ago, I was given twenty thousand pounds as a Trustee for a young man who is still a minor. He is to receive his inheritance when he comes of age in February of eighteen fifty. Till then, I must pay him an income of six hundred pounds, half–yearly. But—

LUKER
But you went and squandered the whole Trust on your little mistress, didn't you?

GODFREY
You don't understand! She's everything to me. All that I've done, I've done for her.

LUKER
To keep her in the style to which she's grown accustomed, eh? So, how deep in are you?

GODFREY
I need three hundred pounds at once, and twenty thousand a year from February.

LUKER
And if you can't raise the money?

GODFREY
I am a ruined man.

CUFF
(To the audience) He proposed to Miss Rachel on her birthday, but she refused him. At dinner, Mr. Blake angered Dr. Candy, and the doctor played a practical joke in return, with a dose of opium from Lady Verinder's medicine chest. He entrusted it to Mr. Ablewhite, who was only too ready to join the prank.

(GODFREY, CANDY, JENNINGS, FRANKLIN, RACHEL and LADY JULIA replay the following scene)

JENNINGS

(To CANDY) I fear, sir, we'll get wet through and through on the way home.

CANDY
(Laughing) Nonsense! A doctor's skin is waterproof! You should know that, Jennings. *(He shakes hands with GODFREY. We see now that he slips GODFREY a phial of opium, which GODFREY conceals. CANDY crosses to LADY JULIA)* My thanks for an... unforgettable evening, Lady Julia.

(CANDY shakes hands with LADY JULIA and exits. The scene shifts ahead)

CUFF
(To the audience) He joined Betteredge in persuading Mr. Blake to have a drink.

GODFREY
I must say, Franklin, you look like death itself. Take some brandy or something before bed.

FRANKLIN
No, no; I'm fine.

BETTEREDGE
Master Franklin, I do advise your having a nightcap. You must get some rest tonight.

FRANKLIN
Very well. Send some brandy and water up to my room.

(FRANKLIN exits. BETTEREDGE pours a brandy and water into a glass, hands it to GODFREY, and exits. GODFREY empties the contents of the phial into the glass and exits after FRANKLIN)

CUFF

(To the audience) After slipping the laudanum into Blake's grog, Ablewhite went to his room. But his money troubles kept him awake. Then he heard Blake in the corridor.

(GODFREY peeks out his door and sees FRANKLIN in the hallway in an opium haze, candle in hand)

FRANKLIN
How do I know? The Indians may be hidden in the house.

CUFF
(To the audience) Till then, he had supposed the laudanum to be a harmless practical joke. But it seemed to have taken some serious effect. Ablewhite followed Blake to the sitting room, and watched him take the diamond. And he saw Miss Verinder as well. He was so surprised by these proceedings that he was unable to return to his room before....

(FRANKLIN collides with GODFREY. Drowsily, he presses the Moonstone into GODFREY's hand)

FRANKLIN
Take it away. Not safe here. *(Stumbling away)* I can't do it. Can't feel my feet under me...

(FRANKLIN exits, leaving GODFREY holding the Moonstone. GODFREY crosses to LUKER)

GODFREY
So, I returned to my room with the diamond.

LUKER
What was your plan?

GODFREY

I had no plan, except to wait and see what happened in the morning. But the next day, Franklin was ignorant of what he had done. And Rachel seemed resolved to say nothing.

LUKER
So you could keep the diamond with impunity. Tell you what: I'll take the stone on pledge, but I'm not giving you twenty thousand for it. All you'll get from me is the three hundred you need now. And you'll be grateful for it, won't you? Because I'm going to keep my mouth shut about what I just heard. Then we can see where things stand when we reclaim it in a year.

(LUKER exits as FRANKLIN enters and joins CUFF)

CUFF
(To the audience) A series of desperate marriage proposals followed, and failed, until Ablewhite was left five thousand pounds by an elderly admirer. That legacy led to his death. He used it to go to Amsterdam and make arrangements for selling the Moonstone. He came back in disguise, and redeemed the diamond, on the appointed day.

FRANKLIN
(To the audience) If he had gotten away with it, there would have been time before February to safely dispose of the stone. But that never came to pass.

CUFF
(To the audience) And that is the tale of Godfrey Ablewhite.

(GODFREY and CUFF exit)
FRANKLIN

(To the audience, taking up the letter he set aside at the top of the play) Now then, the final word on the Moonstone goes to the esteemed foreign traveler, Mr. Murthwaite, whose tale is told in this letter, received many months later.

(BETTEREDGE enters)

BETTEREDGE
(To the audience) Master Franklin, if I may. There is a fact of family history here which I won't allow you to pass over.

FRANKLIN
Of course, Betteredge. Together, you and Mr. Murthwaite shall bring us all, at last, fully into the light.

(MURTHWAITE appears. As he speaks, the INDIANS enact the ceremony described)

MURTHWAITE
(To the audience) Dear sir, about a fortnight ago, I found myself in the wild regions of Kathiawar and discovered many people headed to the city of Somnath. The numbers grew until the throng had swollen to thousands.

BETTEREDGE
(To the audience) Do not suppose I have any more to say concerning the Indian diamond. I hold that jewel in abhorrence. No, I am here to inform you of the marriage of Miss Rachel and Mr. Franklin.

(RACHEL and FRANKLIN are seen being married as the INDIAN ceremony continues. Both ceremonies play out simultaneously, the Western strangely mirroring the Eastern)

BETTEREDGE
(To the audience) The happy event took place at our house in the dying days of eighteen 'forty–nine.

MURTHWAITE
(To the audience) Atop a hill, at midnight, I witnessed a remarkable ceremony. Imagine the moonlight of the East, pouring in unclouded glory over all...

BETTEREDGE
(To the audience) Imagine the red rays of the dusky sun streaming through our chapel windows...

MURTHWAITE
(To the audience) Thousands of people dressed in white, lit by wild red torch flames...

BETTEREDGE
(To the audience) Hundreds of well–wishers from near and far...

MURTHWAITE
(To the audience) And then imagine my surprise when I saw, leading the ceremony, three men to whom I had spoken at Lady Verinder's house. These Brahmins, who had forfeited their caste in service to their god, were to part that night in three separate directions. Never more would they see each other, or their families, or their homeland, from that day till death.

FRANKLIN & RACHEL
Till death do us part.

(The INDIANS return the Moonstone to the forehead of the moon god idol, where it glows once more. Then they bid farewell with an embrace while FRANKLIN and RACHEL kiss)

BETTEREDGE

(To the audience) Family festivals having been rare since my mistress's death, I own to taking a drop too much on the strength of it. If you have ever done the same thing yourself you will understand. After the wretchedest year of mistrust and confusion, the young master and dear Rachel were finally one, heart and soul: man and wife at last.

MURTHWAITE

(To the audience) And there, soaring above us, dark and awful in the light of heaven, was the god of the Moon. And on its forehead gleamed the yellow diamond which had last shone on me from a young girl's dress! Yes! After eight centuries, the Moonstone looks once more over the city where its story began. So the years pass, and so revolve the cycles of time. What will be the next adventures of the Moonstone? Who can tell?

BLACKOUT

END OF PLAY

ABOUT THE AUTHOR

A close friend of Charles Dickens', **William "Wilkie" Collins** was one of the best known, best loved, and best paid of Victorian fiction writers. Inventor of the "Sensation Novel", he penned 30 novels, over 60 short stories, and 14 plays. His first great success was THE WOMAN IN WHITE, followed quickly by NO NAME, ARMADALE, and then in 1868 THE MOONSTONE.

Described by T.S. Eliot as "the first and greatest of the English detective novels", THE MOONSTONE was hailed by readers and critics, one of whom observed that "not a window is opened, a door shut, or a nose blown, but, depend upon it, the act will have something to do with the end of the book."

Much of THE MOONSTONE was written while Collins was consuming large quantities of opium to alleviate the pain of gout. His own experiences of the drug are portrayed in the character of Ezra Jennings, the incurable addict who receives relief from pain at the cost of hideous nightmares.

ABOUT THE PLAYWRIGHT

Robert Kauzlaric has written more than a dozen theatrical adaptations which have been performed in nearly forty states across the U.S., as well as in Ireland, England, and Canada.

The New York Times called his adaptation of THE TRUE STORY OF THE 3 LITTLE PIGS! "One of the best children's shows of the year." His version of H.G. Wells' THE ISLAND OF DR. MOREAU received five of Chicago's Non-Equity Jeff Awards, including New Adaptation and Best Production; his adaptation of Neil Gaiman's NEVERWHERE received the Non-Equity Jeff Award for New Adaptation; and his version of Oscar Wilde's THE PICTURE OF DORIAN GRAY was nominated for New Adaptation. He was commissioned by the Illinois Shakespeare Festival in 2010 to produce a new adaptation of Dumas' THE THREE MUSKETEERS, and two of his plays have been published by Playscripts, Inc.

ABOUT LIFELINE THEATRE

Lifeline Theatre is driven by a passion for story. The ensemble process supports writers in the development of literary adaptations and new work, while their theatrical and educational programs foster a lifelong engagement with literature and the arts. A cultural anchor of the Rogers Park neighborhood in Chicago, they are committed to deepening their connection to an ever-growing family of artists and audiences, both near and far.

Lifeline Theatre's history of extraordinary world premiere adaptations includes MainStage productions of PRIDE & PREJUDICE, THE OVERCOAT, THE LEFT HAND OF DARKNESS, THE TALISMAN RING, JANE EYRE, CAT'S CRADLE, AROUND THE WORLD IN 80 DAYS, THE KILLER ANGELS, A ROOM WITH A VIEW, THE ISLAND OF DR. MOREAU, THE MARK OF ZORRO, MARIETTE IN ECSTASY, NEVERWHERE, THE MOONSTONE, WATERSHIP DOWN, and THE COUNT OF MONTE CRISTO.

Lifeline also produced world premiere adaptations of J. R. R. Tolkein's THE LORD OF THE RINGS trilogy (THE FELLOWSHIP OF THE RING, THE TWO TOWERS, AND THE RETURN OF THE RING) and four installments of the Dorothy L. Sayers Lord Peter Wimsey mysteries (WHOSE BODY?, STRONG POISON, GAUDY NIGHT, and BUSMAN'S HONEYMOON).

Family MainStage productions have included A WRINKLE IN TIME, LIZARD MUSIC, THE SNARKOUT BOYS AND THE AVACADO OF DEATH, THE PHANTOM TOLLBOOTH, JOURNEY OF THE SPARROWS, THE SILVER CHAIR, JOHNNY TREMAIN, and TREASURE ISLAND.

In 1986 Lifeline inaugurated its KidSeries program. Productions have included MR. POPPER'S PENGUINS, MIKE MULLIGAN AND HIS STEAM SHOVEL, BUNNICULA, JAMES AND THE GIANT PEACH, THE STORY OF FERDINAND, MRS. PIGGLE-WIGGLE, MY FATHER'S DRAGON, CLICK CLACK MOO: COWS THAT TYPE, THE STINKY CHEESE MAN, DUCK FOR PRESIDENT, THE TRUE STORY OF THE 3 LITTLE PIGS!, THE VELVETEEN RABBIT, THE LAST OF THE DRAGONS, and ARNIE THE DOUGHNUT.

Plays commissioned by Lifeline Theatre have gone on to publication, numerous regional and national tours, and to more than a hundred subsequent productions across over forty U.S. states, five Canadian provinces, as well as in England and Ireland.

FOR MORE INFORMATION
VISIT WWW.LIFELINETHEATRE.COM

lifeline
THEATRE
Big Stories, Up Close

Other Plays From SORDELET INK

The Woman in White
by Robert Kauzlaric
adapted from the novel by Wilkie Collins

The Count of Monte Cristo
by Christoper M Walsh
adapted from the novel by Alexandre Dumas

A Tale of Two Cities
by Christoper M Walsh
adapted from the novel by Charles Dickens

Season on the Line
by Shawn Pfautsch
adapted from Herman Melville's Moby-Dick

Hatfield & McCoy
by Shawn Pfautsch

It Came From Mars
by Joseph Zettelmaier

Ebeneezer - A Christmas Play
by Joseph Zettelmaier

Eve of Ides
by David Blixt

www.ingramcontent.com/pod-product-compliance
Lightning Source LLC
Chambersburg PA
CBHW060155050426
42446CB00013B/2842